Unlocking the Numbers

Unlocking the Numbers

An LDS Perspective on Scriptural Use of Numbers

George M. Peacock

CFI
Springville, Utah

ISBN: 1-55517-825-1
v.1

Published by CFI
an imprint of Cedar Fort, Inc.
925 N. Main Springville, Utah, 84663
www.cedarfort.com

Distributed by:

Cover design by Nicole Williams
Cover design © 2005 by Lyle Mortimer

Printed in the United States of America
10 9 8 7 6 5 4 3 2 1

Printed on acid-free paper

Table of Contents

Introduction

Symbols and Their Use

Symbols are the instruments of all communication, the building blocks of all alphabets. Symbols are the marks that are printed, carved, and painted, the motions that are performed and displayed. By their function or position, these haphazard combinations of lines imitate something of significance. Many times, symbols trigger both emotion and memory, and in all cases, they stand for something. Symbols communicate, record, emphasize, and illustrate.

A relationship always exists between a symbol and what the symbol represents, a relationship built upon association, resemblance, or function. A symbol often represents something invisible—tangible evidence of the intangible. For example, the circle formed with the thumb and index finger, with the remaining fingers staying upright is the universal symbol that everything is okay.

A symbol can thus serve as a simple representation of something much more complex than the symbol itself. The mere shape of a traffic sign, with its color and design, evokes feelings about the law and its consequences without ever displaying the entire written law or describing the ramifications of certain actions.

The shaking of a mother's head and the movement of her finger are reminders to her child of lessons taught—lessons that likely have included instructions in morals and values.

The figures most often chosen as symbols are things commonly understood by everyone—functional, ordinary things surrounding us that we often depend on. The most traditional symbols include parts of the human body, colors that exist in nature, or elements of geography, science, metals, animals, and foods. Languages utilize alphabet figures; these too are symbols. Numbers are symbols that establish an order or an amount. Musical scores employ notes and bars as symbols. In addition, people seldom speak without also relying on facial and body expressions to convey ideas and emotions that go beyond spoken words.

Symbolism in Scriptural Texts

God uses symbols prominently as He communicates to mortal man. Prophets, who speak for God, employ symbolism in their prophecies, exhortations, and teachings. In matters religious and spiritual, symbols are used to excite the mind, amplify the emotions, or expand understanding. These processes are generally employed when earthly things are compared to things of heavenly significance. Such earthly things, chosen as symbols, might be as small as a mote or speck in an eye, yet they represent something as complex and immense as personal sins that keep one from entering the kingdom of heaven.

When searching for meaning and application in scripture study, we must be aware that writers of scriptural texts employ much symbolic language. The reader of scripture may not always recognize symbolic forms of communication. However, if such forms were employed by the authors to add meaning and emphasis to what they wrote, such meaning and emphasis only come to the reader when recognized and understood. And even when recognition and understanding take place, the heart is where change has the most effect.

Identifying and understanding the forms of symbolic writing is a constant challenge to anyone who engages in this effort. In short, symbolic language is unavoidable in scripture study. The reader is constantly introduced to parables, allegories, hyperbole, types, and shadows. These forms compare things that are real and literal with things that are figurative and spiritual.

Numbers As Symbols

Numbers are classic symbolic images often used in scriptural text. One reason is that numbers are precise and definite; they are exact. For example, the very essence of the number four is that it is not the same as the number three. Three never can become four unless one is added to it. Because of these distinct differences, we see another reason why numbers make excellent symbols: numbers have a size, position, and character that give them a figurative essence as well as a literal one. Because of inherently unique elements, each number delivers a message that it alone can give.

Recognizing the unique characteristics of a number generally leads to an understanding of how it can be used as a symbol and, thus, how it can communicate a figurative message. For example, characteristics of the number one, such as size and position, dictate that the number one always comes before any other whole number. When a prophet wants people to place something first in their lives or in their thoughts, he might use the number one, suggesting that nothing else should be placed before whatever he associates with that number.

Similarly, the nature of the number ten makes it the only number that can be squared and cubed simply by adding zeros, making it unique. The scope and intent of this book is to consider the symbolic nature of certain numbers that have been used by God and by authors of scriptural texts.

In our culture, using numbers as symbols is common. Countless people fall in love with *the one*. That two may become one is every married couple's hope and dream, and when we are deeply happy, we often say we are in seventh heaven.

How many lives does a cat have? Ships are sent to the deep six. Someone says that a certain thing will never happen, not even in a hundred years. We use these idioms to convey messages that are not literal but are related to the nature of the number chosen and used.

Engaged couples avoid getting married on any Friday falling

on the thirteenth. In fact, when we say Friday the thirteenth, we expect most people to understand that this is a day laden with bad luck and superstition. Why? Simply because the number thirteen has, for a long time, been thought of as unlucky.

On some roller coasters, the cars are numbered so they can be referenced and maintained. On one such roller coaster, the thirteenth seat or car had no number. The reason, reported the operators, was that people often refused to sit in it when it bore the unlucky number. Thus, the operators left the thirteenth seat unnumbered. The ride itself took you to the brink of disaster, so why add more risk by sitting in an unlucky seat?

In describing beauty and attractiveness, people sometimes rate others as a ten. That is all that needs to be said. The assessment is clear and it needs no other explanation or support; the message is communicated much more than simply the small word or number ten. Ten is also a symbol.

Certain numbers are like that. They often suggest a message beyond their literal numerical value. For example, a baker's dozen is an interesting term. In decades past, bakers surprised valued customers who purchased a dozen pastries. When the customers arrived home and counted their purchases, they often discovered one extra treat. The baker had added an extra pastry in case one was not quite right or simply to ensure that his customers were getting their money's worth. Hence, a baker's dozen is more than twelve but is still called a dozen.

Are Numbers Literal or Figurative?

Numbers are used to convey concepts in at least four ways:

1. The literal use of the number, as an amount or numerical value.
2. The position indicated by the number, such as, "You are fifth in line."
3. The number of times something is listed or item- ized within a defined text.

4. The symbolic idea associated with the number.

Most often, a number is used for its literal numerical value. However, occasionally a number has symbolical meaning, even if it can, or should be, considered literal. Such instances include making comparisons, giving descriptions, providing series and lists, repeating words and phrases, or exaggerating numbers.

Examples of exaggeration in the English language are many. When we want to communicate that someone has been told something enough times that the meaning should be clear, we might say, "I've told you a million times." If the statement is taken literally, then we must conclude that someone has been told something one thousand thousand times!

We might also say, "This thing weighs a ton" as we grunt and groan to heft something into the air. If that were actually the case, we should join the Olympic weight-lifting team! When we use phrases or idioms such as these, clearly the message is more important than the actual number. Some of these idioms are not only exaggerated but are also impossible.

When we are asked to give 110 percent, that can be terribly confusing. Isn't 100 percent all that is possible to give? Yet, if we think about it figuratively, a powerful idea enters our mind. Figuratively, if we give 110 percent, we may literally come close to giving 100 percent effort.

These examples illustrate why it is critical to ask ourselves, whenever numbers are used in communication, "Which is intended? The literal number, a symbolic message, or both?"

When we want to know the real significance of a number, start by looking at the way the number is used. Next, examine all the instances in which the number is mentioned as well as applied. Further, carefully study the nature of the number. Ask, "What is unique about it?" "What can it do that nothing else can do?" "What can it do better than anything else?" Also investigate how people from the past have used the number.

This kind of thought and study leads to the best possible interpretation of the number. It also helps determine if the number has been or is currently used as a symbol.

Another key we can use when deciding whether to take a number literally or figuratively is to be aware of the idiomatic patterns used by those whose writings we are considering. This book deals with declarations made by God and by prophets who speak God's words. These prophets teach as well as prophesy, and when they do so, they use the language of their day, often relying on figurative expressions. Good teachers and prophets use images that depict more than their literal meaning. They paint pictures in the minds of their listeners, hoping to move them to feeling, and then to action.

Eastern vs. Western Thought

In Western culture and thought, we use symbols a great deal in our thinking and writing. However, we don't seem to use symbols as frequently as did the writers in the Bible who lived in Eastern culture. Why is this so?

The most-used explanation for this difference arises from comparing the characteristics of Eastern, or Oriental, thinking with the characteristics of those of Western, or Occidental, thinking and writing. Sidney B. Sperry notes that Eastern peoples are much more prone to use imagery than are Western peoples.

He writes: "We ofttimes read our Bible as though its peoples were English or American and interpret their sayings in terms of our own background and psychology. But the Bible is actually an Oriental book. It was written centuries ago by Oriental people and primarily for Oriental people. . . .

"It may be of interest to contrast the speech of modern and ancient Palestinians with our own. In thought and speech the Oriental is an artist; the Occidental, on the other hand, may be thought of as an architect. When speaking, the Oriental paints a scene whose total effect is true, but the details may be inaccurate; the Occidental tends to draw diagrams accurate in detail ("Hebrew Manners and Customers," *Ensign* May 1972, 29–30).

If we find numbers used as symbols in our own Western culture, we should expect to find much more of this in writings produced by Eastern authors. Recognition of such abundant use of numbers as symbols may be difficult for a Western reader of Eastern texts. Little wonder that it is such a challenge for those of us in the West to understand writings so far removed from us culturally and chronologically.

Use of Numbers in the Hebrew and Greek Alphabets

Those who speak and write in English use a system of numbers separate and distinct from the English alphabet. This is not the case for those who used Hebrew or Greek in biblical times. Their system of counting and numbering utilized the same alphabet as used for words. In other words, the letters of the alphabet each had an assigned numerical value in addition to their alphabetic use. Knowing whether to think of a letter as a number as opposed to using it as a language character depended on the way it was used within the text.

Sometimes the use of numbers in this manner could reflect both a numerical and alphabetical value. We call this *dualism*. But for those who use an alphabet for language and a separate set of symbols for numbers, it can be most confusing. We may find it difficult to interchange the message of an alphabet letter with its value, let alone comprehend the dualism that possibly exists within the use of such letters.

However, to those who wrote and spoke biblical languages, this practice was basic and elementary, almost instinctive. The actual process of giving an amount or value count to alphabet letters is called *gematria*, which means "measuring." Because biblical writers practiced this, it is also referred to as biblical gematria.

Biblical authors thought, spoke, and wrote with an interchangeable system that many times combined both numbers and words. Because words contained several letters, words were thought of as numbers because they had a weight or total of the numerical values of all the letters contained in each word.

Many Westerners are suspicious of this process and feel that it is similar to numerology. However, a definite distinction can be made between these two ideas. Gematria uses numbers to communicate a message; numerology uses a person's date of birth to predict future events in that person's life.

Biblical Gematria

Ed. F. Vallowe gave an assessment and definition of biblical gematria:

> Biblical gematria is a little different from biblical mathematics. Gematria has to do with the letters of the original Hebrew and Greek words throughout the whole Bible. Originally, both the Hebrew and Greek languages did not have symbols (1, 2, 3, 4) to represent numbers, like we do in our own language. The way their numbers are represented is through the use of their alphabets. This is why in the whole Bible, you find numbers written out as words instead of using symbols. Example: The number 1 is actually the first letter of either the Hebrew or Greek alphabet. The symbol 1 is actually the Hebrew letter "Aleph" and the Greek letter "Alpha." The number 2 is "Bet" or "Beta," and so on. Each letter of the Hebrew and Greek alphabet also represents a number. So, when you look at the words in scripture, you are also looking as a very intricately woven set of "spirit numbers" just sitting there, waiting for us to discover.
>
> Each letter of each word has a numeric value. This value is called weight. This is why the book of Revelation says that those who have wisdom are to count the number of the beast. Since each letter of the alphabet has a numeric value, this means each word of the Bible has a numeric value. The same is for each word, each

sentence, and each paragraph. And words that have the same numeric value or weight are considered to be connected somehow. (*Biblical Mathematics, Keys to Scripture Numerics*, 21–22)

Jesus used the idea of gematria when he indicated that he was "Alpha and Omega" (Revelation 22:13). Alpha was the first letter of the alphabet and omega was the last letter of the alphabet used by those to whom he was speaking.

Understanding this process helps immensely with certain scriptural anomalies. One of the best examples of values assigned to letters of the alphabet appears in the first chapter of Matthew. The beginning of a declaration as significant and singular as this shouldn't have just a common beginning. It should be captivating and concise.

However, an English reader of this chapter may be tempted to skip over it in order to get to the "good stuff." In fact, Matthew's genealogy may appear to be very boring: so and so is the father of so and so, and he had a son of . . . . You may conclude that it is not captivating at all and wonder why in the world Matthew started off his gospel in such a manner.

Maybe someone informs you that you are reading the lineage that preceded Jesus in his mortal life. However, you will find a similar lineage in Luke, and if you compare the two, you will find that they are not identical. Maybe they are not both the lineage of Jesus; maybe one is of Mary and the other of Joseph. However, if you study them carefully, you will notice a number amid the names listed in the Matthew account, a number not included in Luke's record.

Maybe you should count the names. Matthew 1:17 gives the summary of what you should find: "So all the generations from Abraham to David are fourteen generations; and from David until the carrying away into Babylon are fourteen generations; and from the carrying away into Babylon unto Christ are fourteen generations."

If you count the names within each of the epics mentioned,

you will not actually find fourteen for each one. Furthermore, if you carefully check the genealogical record contained within the Old Testament, you will note that some names do not appear in Matthew's pedigree list. This is in addition to the differences in pedigree between Matthew and Luke. To find the reasoning behind this seeming oversight, and to recognize the power with which Matthew begins his testimony, we need to look at the gematria for the name of David.

What is significant about the name of David? God promises that through the lineage of David, a descendant of Judah, would come the Messiah (Genesis 49:10). Therefore, the name of David held enormous significance to the people of Matthew's day. Not only was David the greatest king in Israel's history, but his was also the lineage to watch in order to recognize the deliverer and king who would come to a people desperately needing salvation and leadership.

In Hebrew, vowels are not written, and the sound of those letters are resupplied when spoken. When you remove the vowels from David's written name, you have DVD. Using gemetria, you can determine the numerical value for his name. The fourth letter in the Hebrew alphabet is the same as the corresponding fourth letter in the English alphabet. It is the letter *D* and is sounded or called Dalet. Both D's in the name David would be given the numerical value of four.

Now consider the *V.* The letter is Vav, and it is the sixth letter in both the Hebrew and Greek alphabets. Its numerical value, of course, is six. So the total of the four, six, and four is fourteen! That is the number for the name of David (Walter C. Kaiser, *"Why Don't Bible Genealogies Match Up?"*).

Matthew was writing his gospel to the Jews, and so he wrote something that would make them think and take notice. The significance of the name David was far beyond what the names Lincoln, Washington, Jefferson, and Jackson mean to Americans. By using that one word or number, Matthew was saying that whoever was at the end of that lineage would be a king to them. He expected his readers to understand this double meaning.

Compare this concept to Luke's genealogical list. Luke wrote his gospel to a friend who was undoubtedly a Gentile, a man who would not care about the name of David the same way a Jew or Israelite would. Therefore, Luke doesn't mention the number fourteen.

Additionally it appears that Matthew omitted some of the names of Joseph's lineage so that the number of generations equaled fourteen. He was more intent on having the number fourteen be eminent than having the record be historically accurate. Thus the difference between the lineage written by Matthew and that written by Luke (see Robert L. Millett, "The Birth of the Messiah: A Closer Look at the Infancy Narrative of Matthew," 1980 CES Symposium presentation [Provo, Utah: BYU Presss, 1980]).

A visit to the birthplace of Jesus allows us to observe the significance of the number fourteen. Visitors going into the Church of the Nativity in Bethlehem of Judea are told that the structure has been built over the very spot, the stable where Joseph took Mary, his wife, because there was no room in the inn.

Those who want to see this spot walk below the main floor, down some steps, and into the Grotto of the Nativity. There you see a manger hewn from native stone that has been placed at the locale where, it is said, the birth of Jesus took place.

In front and center of the manger is a hole in the stone, a perfectly round hole that marks the spot. Surrounding the spot are containers of oil, symbols for light and richness of life. The whole grotto is full of other symbols, but you notice emanating from the hole in the stone rays made of precious metals. These rays resemble spires of a star; they uniformly radiate from the hole all the way around it. You now know the significance of the spot represented by the hole near the manger. It is the place where the child of Joseph and son of Mary—both descendants of David, king of Israel—was born.

You would expect an inscription or identifier declaring whose birthplace this is. And then you notice it. You count the number of rays or spires that radiate from the hole; they number fourteen, the number for David! This is the spot where the Messiah, who was to be a descendant of Abraham, Judah, and David, was supposedly born. To descendants of these patriarchs, the number fourteen is as meaningful as the thirteen stripes and fifty stars are to an American who pledges allegiance to the flag. Christians, who wanted Jews and all others to know that Jesus was the fulfillment of the promises made to Abraham, Judah, and David, made the hole in the stone with the fourteen rays coming from it. It is a declaration of tremendous significance, a small symbol that represents a momentous concept. But that is what symbols do. And numbers used as symbols do it especially well.

Amazing and Tedious Studies

Many biblical scholars, both living and long dead, have examined the use of numbers as symbols in the books of the Bible. The results of many of these examinations have been published. Most of these significant studies were conducted long before the availability of the computer, and their magnitude amazes the mind.

The countless hours needed to make the assessments and conclusions are staggering, to say the least. These scholars would not only need to be familiar with the texts but also would have to review and count, deduct and conclude, while examining passages for every nuance of interpretation, both for doctrine as well as historical setting. Published reports of their findings have been reviewed in numerous settings. Some researchers have published books as well as articles and reports, in addition to many entries in biblical dictionaries.

Access to these documents has been somewhat limited until the recent proliferation of information available on the Internet. Not only can computers verify these reports, but they can also be used to examine the scriptural texts themselves. Computers can even do the searching, counting, and comparing, without the tedious time-consuming effort of the past. These searches and counts can now be done instantly with the click of a mouse. The most difficult task is to generate a proper query for the computer to search.

I have tried to review these sources. But without the groundwork of the early scholars already mentioned, queries and searches would be less meaningful, and conclusions would be far fewer.

Studies have sometimes identified codes and mystic applications. With the new data from this "modern revelation"—the computer—as well as the increased volume of material to consider, some of these applications may even seem out of place. My position is that we should not be ignorant of the fact that numbers were used in the writing of scriptural texts. Further, we should strive to understand what the writers actually intended. Unfortunately, many investigators of these codes and systems have gone from ignorance to total obsession. They count every word, letter, phrase, and sentence as equally valuable, with all manner of esoteric expectations. They seem to feel that every writer used the same techniques and that events past and modern are embodied in these codes and systems. Such expectations may go well beyond the intentions of some scriptural authors.

What This Study Is Not

This study, therefore, is not a study of *numerology,* or attributing an inherent value to numbers. Numerology is not just a common study of numbers. It is an ancient science, so called by Pythagoras, a Greek philosopher, who established a university in 532 B.C. for those who sought to free the mind of ignorance and discover the meaning of life and love. Part of this discovery was to identify a person's starting point or life number, a number determined by adding the digits contained within an individual's birth date. When the sum of these digits is reduced to a single digit, it is called a life number.

According to believers in numerology, this life number brings to people the experiences that have been chosen for this life. The number can thus be considered to have a metaphysical influence over people throughout their live. It makes life's little ups and downs more bearable if a person reminds himself that this life number was assigned at birth and controls many of the things that will happen in his lifetime. This number can't be changed because the date of birth is set.

I do not intend that this book be associated with numerology in any way. I also hope that any findings noted herein will not be used to further numerology. I do not profess a belief in numerology, and I do not want any findings shared in this study to be used to further that science.

I do, however, recognize gematria, a technique clearly used by some recorders of scripture to add emphasis to their message. Ancient prophets and writers employed this process in their culture. They also memorized oral histories. Techniques such as gematria were helpful in memorizing and reciting oral histories as well as written ones.

Despite my belief in this process, however, I think some gematria goes beyond the intended mark in the geometric assessments and assurances some students of scripture have attached to scriptural accounts. The accounting of how many times certain words and numbers are used in scriptural texts does not consider the variables of translation, inclusion, or additional versions of the books of scripture. And just because a student of these sacred writings finds, by count or definition, an embedded number does not necessarily mean that the author intended it to be used as a symbol or figurative key.

When considering gematria and numerology, we should note that some scholars even combine the two; some have even stated that biblical gematria is Hebrew numerology. This suggests that one is equal to the other, and that if one is viable, the other must also be based upon truth.

Such an assessment should be considered with caution. Gematria was a known practice in Hebrew custom and thought. Numerology is only a theory and a developed process some have applied to scriptural writing after the fact. It didn't come about until the sixth century b.c. The use of numerology by the authors of scripture is only a supposition by those who make such an assertion. Increased clarification and identification of how these numbers are used will place them more in the realm of symbols than in the realm of mythical predictors of life and its happenstance.

Scope of This Study

Believers in The Church of Jesus Christ of Latter-day Saints study and adhere to the Bible and to volumes of scripture considered companions to the Bible, which have been published in modern times. These additional books of scripture include the following:

- The Book of Mormon—A book containing histories of people, many of which parallel biblical histories in time and patterns. The histories contained therein originate in the lands of the Bible but take place somewhere in the Americas. These people had prophets who spoke, wrote, taught, warned, and pointed all their doctrine to the same God of the Bible. This record was first published in 1830 in New York. It is considered scripture by millions and is written for study and direction. This volume is more than five hundred pages in length.

- The Doctrine and Covenants—A book that contains recorded revelations received by prophets, beginning in 1823 and moving to the last insertion dated 1978. These revelations are also considered scripture and comprise nearly three hundred pages of detailed text.

- The Pearl of Great Price—A book that contains a combination of ancient as well as modern prophetic writings. Likewise this volume is formatted for notation and study by being divided into chapters and verses. It contains sixty-one pages of text.

When adding the number of pages of scriptural text contained in these three additional volumes (nearly nine hundred pages) to the number of pages of text contained in the Bible (nearly sixteen hundred pages), the scope of material open for examination in the search for numbers and their symbolic use in scripture is greatly enlarged. What an inviting venue for the searcher of scriptural insights, not just in the amount of additional scripture to examine but also in the change from a biblical setting—in time, geography, and culture—to others that can be observed and compared.

All these scriptural volumes profess the same doctrines and faith in the same God; the revelations have the same God as their source. It should also be of great interest to see if the numbers used as symbols in the Bible are used in the same manner in these additional volumes of scripture as well.

The conclusions and findings of this book will be of interest to those who profess belief in all four books. I analyze scriptural passages from each of them, treating passages from the newer scriptural volumes in the same manner as biblical ones. Quotations and observations from prophets, living and dead, who have touched on this subject are noted. In addition, quotations from credible publications that contain teachings of those who believe in all these scriptural volumes are included with their sources. These may or may not be familiar to those who are acquainted only with the Bible. Some familiarity with all four scriptural volumes, and with these additional publications, is assumed in this study. Belief in the prophets who brought forth and recorded these scriptural texts is likewise a given.

My findings, conclusions, and deductions should not to be considered doctrine or policy of The Church of Jesus Christ of Latter-day Saints. I am personally responsible for all these.

I recognize that this book is neither exhaustive nor final. The numbers chosen to be examined include the most commonly used that are considered symbols. Not all are of equal significance;

however, the consecutive numbers from one to twelve are the main focus. Additional numbers are also considered, including the numbers forty and seventy.

1

The Number That Excludes All Others

As we consider the number one, we must let the nature of the symbol teach us, as must be done with all symbols. That is one of the strongest methods of discovering the meaning of each and every symbol (see Gerald N. Lund, "Understanding Scriptural Symbols," *Ensign*, October 1986, 23).

Question: What is the nature of the number one?"

Answer: The number one comes first in the numbering system, and nothing can come before it.

These characteristics are unique to this number. The feature of being first is a primary basis for its use as a symbol. In addition to being first, the number also stands alone, by itself. The idea of one indicates that there is not another. There is no other in any category or classification. By itself, without the existence of any other number, the number one can't be compared with anything else and nothing else can encroach on its position of prominence. It is clear that this number has much potential use as a symbol. In life and in theology, one thing in particular often compares to the number one. It comes first; it stands alone and can't be compared to anything else. What is this thing or being? God.

Not only does the number one come first in the system of numbers, but it is the only number that can be divided or multiplied by any other number and not become another number. This can suggest that God is in everything and there is not anything save God is in it (D&C 88:7–13). It also suggests that God is unchangeable. Just like the number one, God stands supreme. When thinking of God, speaking of God, worshiping God, there is no one beside Him. God stands alone. These concepts are infused in Deuteronomy 6:4: "The Lord our God is one Lord."

Some will read scriptural statements referencing God that use the number one to symbolize Him with a Western mind-set. They look for details of how many members are in the godhead or which member of the godhead should be the object of adulation. Easterners, or Orientals, who generally look for the total picture more than the details, will read it and be more apt to have thoughts of the majesty of God, His wonder and His might. They will read that beside Him there is no one else to whom to look for redemption. They will stand like an observer of a great painting or a large tapestry, in awe, because they see the picture painted in the brush strokes of an artist who is trying to project an impression and a feeling rather than just to communicate a count or amount.

Many have appraised a verse in the book of Isaiah seeking doctrinal clarification of the godhead. The answer as to how many Gods there are, or which God is referred to, should not come from reading this verse. The theme of the verse is the exclusion of false gods: "I, even I, am the Lord; and beside me there is no savior" (Isaiah 43:11).

Those who believe that there is only one God depend heavily on this verse. However, with the idea of exclusion in mind, we should understand that Isaiah was not attempting to tell us the number of gods. He was simply saying that there is no other God to whom we should look for salvation. All three members of the godhead are involved in such work. They alone fit in the category of who can and will save us.

The number one has for its fundamental idea this concept of exclusion. If you want to plant an image for number one in your mind, try this: Close your eyes and think of a large piece of pure white paper. There is not a single mark of any kind on it. Now mentally place a mark or dot on the paper. Just one dot. As you think about this image, what comes to your mind? Is there anything like that dot? If there is not another one, it has to be first. If there is only one, then you can't compare it to anything else. You can't arrange the dots on the paper in any order because there is only one. There is nothing else in its category, and there is no other category. Therefore, it is exclusive of everything else.

That is the idea associated with the number one—exclusiveness. That is the nature of number one. This is why God is represented so well by this number and why it is such a qualified symbol to represent God. That does not mean that the number one can't be used as a symbol for anything else. If something else is exclusive, first, or unlike anything else, it too could be represented by the number one. So, if we apply its nature and message whenever and wherever we find it in a scriptural text, we learn much about whatever it symbolically represents.

Mytonomy and the Number One

Mytonomy is the practice of giving a person or place a name whose meaning reflects an event or trait associated with that person or place. A biblical example of this is Moses being given his name, which meant "to draw out" (Exodus 2:10). Every Bible reader remembers that Moses was drawn out of the river by the Pharaoh's daughter and she named him and tried to raise him as her own son. She gave him the name, remembering that she had drawn him out of the river.

Another example of mytonomy in the Bible is Benjamin in Genesis 35:18. As his mother, Rachel, was dying, she named her newborn Ben-oni, which translates "son of my sorrow or distress." His father, however, called him Benjamin. Rachel's death was of deepest sorrow to him, not just because she was his wife but also because she had been his first love, even though he had married other wives (see "Mytonomy and the Book of Mormon," *Insights*, June 1984, 1).

Zechariah made excellent use of mytonomy. Making reference to the millennial day and who will reign, he wrote: "And the

Lord shall be king over all the earth: in that day shall there be one Lord, and *his name one*" (Zechariah 14:9; emphasis added).

How better can we describe our God than to use His name? Mytonomy is here combined with numerical symbolism. His name suggests who and what He is. His name uses the numerical value of the digit. His name describes how we should feel about Him. It defines our worship. His name, One, tells where God is to be when we consider our priorities among all other things that matter. He is to be the One, and His name is One.

The Number One—Unity and Exclusion

Concerning the three members of the godhead, Joseph Smith taught, "These three are one; or, in other words, these three constitute the great, matchless, governing and supreme power over all things; by whom all things were created and made that were created and made" (*Lectures on Faith* 5:2).

Commenting on that statement of the oneness of the godhead, Elder Bruce R. McConkie wrote: "In what way are the Father, the Son, and the Holy Ghost one God? Though three persons are involved, they are one supreme presidency, one in creating all things, one in governing the universe with almighty power" (*A New Witness for the Articles of Faith*, 75).

Joseph Smith also wrote:

> And these three constitute the godhead, and are one; the Father and the Son possessing the same mind, the same wisdom, glory, power, and fullness—filling all in all; the Son being filled with the fullness of the mind, glory, and power; or, in other words, the spirit, glory, and power, of the Father, possessing all knowledge and glory, and the same kingdom, sitting at the right hand of power, in the express image and likeness of the Father, mediator for man, being filled with the fullness of the mind of the Father; or, in other words, the Spirit of the Father, which Spirit is shed forth upon

all who believe on his name and keep his commandments. (*Lectures on Faith*, 5:2)

The idea of the members of the godhead being united, of one
mind, power, and purpose, is essential to their being able to reign
supreme. The number one infers sufficiency, power, and omnipo-
tence. It also infers independence, which admits no other. All
these qualities connote exclusiveness.

Exclusiveness is the essence from whence unity comes. If
there is no other thought, work, or plan, then there is unity. Unity
results from exclusiveness. The statement "they are one," referring
to the members of the godhead, speaks more of exclusion than of
unity. Unity can only exist if there is exclusiveness. Eliminating
things, ideas, and concepts is the way to unify. If a group of people
is to become united, differences must be eliminated. Group members must unite in one common quality or objective. They must
exclude anything that would divide or misdirect them.

Unity, therefore, is the product of exclusiveness rather than its
opposite. Becoming united does not bring exclusiveness; exclusiveness brings about unity. Things must be put *outside* the circle
in order for there to be only things *in* the circle that are united.
There can't be total unity until other things are put outside the
circle. Thus, exclusion brings about unity rather than the other
way around. When exclusion has occurred, there is unity and
things are said to be one.

This attribute of being one must ever be present in the members of the godhead, but it should also exist within those who
believe in the godhead and in the work God does. Clearly this is
the message of the intercessory prayer recorded in John: "Neither
pray I for these alone, but for them also which shall believe on
me through their word; that they all may be one; as thou, Father,
art in me, and I in thee, that they also may be one in us: that the
world may believe that thou hast sent me" (John 17:20–21).

If we become one with God, then we have no other god con-
tending for our devotion. And if we all have that same determination, then we too are one. Why are we one? Because we have

unity? Yes, but more so because we are exclusive in our faith, devotion, and worship. We have no faith, devotion, or worship for any other god, whether spiritual or of the flesh.

The Command to Adam and Eve

There exists a message of unity in the following verse, but notice also the idea of exclusiveness: "Therefore shall a man leave his father and his mother, and shall cleave unto his wife: and they shall be one flesh" (Genesis 2:24).

The Savior was asked a question regarding divorce, wherein he was asked, "Is it lawful for a man to put away his wife" (Mark 10:2). He answered the question using the same words cited from Genesis—that they should be one flesh (Mark 10:7). What do these words mean or suggest? Isn't the command to always be united? Realistically, however, a couple will never be totally in unity on every matter. However, two people when married according to the flesh, are to be exclusive.

Could it be that this is the symbolic message of the phrase "one flesh"? Some want to say that it is not symbolic but literal. That is true on occasions. However, the command seems to apply to more than on occasion. If their lives—both sexual and physical—are exclusive of any others, they are following the command to be "one flesh."

Elder A. Theodore Tuttle once said:

> Some worry about the creation of Eve, which is stated symbolically. They miss the message declared by Adam: "This I know now is bone of my bones, and flesh of my flesh" (Moses 3:23). When we look beyond the symbolic teaching, what do we see as the reality? Oneness, harmony, singleness of purpose! What manner of relationship are husband and wife to have? How is the husband to treat his wife, and the wife her husband? What about fidelity, love, unity, priorities, etc.? If we can see the meaning beyond the symbol,

the answers are obvious. ("The Pearl of Great Price as Scripture," 4)

The most effective way and manner to be united with someone or something is to be exclusive in our attention and actions. If there is no other, then there can be unity. If there is another, then there is not unity. Therefore, the members of the godhead are to be one. Similarly, members of the Church are to be one. But, this can be achieved only if there is one doctrine, one faith, and one designated path.

How Many Gods Are There?

The scriptures teach that there are three members of the godhead (Bruce R. McConkie, *Mormon Doctrine*, 319). They are separate and distinct from each other. However, numerous scriptural statements, ancient and modern, indicate that they are one. Note the following:

> And the scribe said unto him, Well, Master, thou hast said the truth: for there is one God; and there is none other but he. (Mark 12:32)

> Seeing it is one God, which shall justify the circumcision by faith, and uncircumcision through faith. (Romans 3:30)

> But to us there is but one God, the Father, of whom are all things, and we in him; and one Lord Jesus Christ, by whom are all things, and we by him. (1 Corinthians 8:6)

Conflict appears to exist between verses such as these and those that indicate there are three members of the godhead. Generally, doctrinal explanations concerning such verses conclude that the three Gods of the godhead are one in purpose and unity, thus justifying scriptural claims. That, at least, seems to be the approach of the Western mind, the mind of the architect, which wants to make all details fit.

However, the Eastern way of thinking should be applied when the oriental writer tries to paint a picture—not necessarily accurate in detail but whose total effect is true—then what should we conclude about the message of the above verses? The answer is that the number of Gods is not as important as what they are— supreme. They are to be considered exclusive of all other gods. That is the message that comes through so strongly in the very first edict from Sinai. "Thou shalt have no other gods before me" (Exodus 20:3). It denotes exclusion and constitutes command- ment number one!

The Book of Mormon Teaches One God

The Book of Mormon handles the oneness of God much like the Bible. Note the following verses:

> They must come according to the words which shall be established by the mouth of the Lamb; and the words of the Lamb shall be made known in the records of thy seed, as well as in the records of the twelve apostles of the Lamb; wherefore they both shall be established in one; for there is *one God* and one Shepherd over all the earth. (1 Nephi 13:41; emphasis added)

> And now, behold, my beloved brethren, this is the way; and there is none other way nor name given under heaven whereby man can be saved in the kingdom of God. And now, behold, this is the doctrine of Christ, and the only and true doctrine of the Father, and of the Son, and of the Holy Ghost, which is *one God*, without end. Amen. (2 Nephi 31:21; emphasis added)

Now Zeezrom said: Is there more than *one God?* And he [Amulek] answered, No. . . . Now Zeezrom said unto the people: See that ye remember these things; for he said there is but *one God;* yet he saith that the Son of God shall come, but he shall not save his people—as though he had authority to command. God (Alma 11:28–29, 35; emphasis added)

And the people went forth and witnessed against them—testifying that they had reviled against the law, and their lawyers and judges of the land, and also of all the people that were in the land; and also testified that there was but *one God,* and that he should send his Son among the people, but he should not save them; and many such things did the people testify against Alma and Amulek. Now this was done before the chief judge of the land. (Alma 14:5; emphasis added)

Now after Alma had spoken these words, they sent forth unto him desiring to know whether they should believe in *one God,* that they might obtain this fruit of which he had spoken, or how they should plant the seed, or the word of which he had spoken, which he said must be planted in their hearts; or in what manner they should begin to exercise their faith. (Alma 33:1; emphasis added)

And he hath brought to pass the redemption of the world, whereby he that is found guiltless before him at the judgment day hath it given unto him to dwell in the presence of God in his kingdom, to sing cease-less praises with the choirs above, unto the Father, and unto the Son, and unto the Holy Ghost, which are *one God,* in a state of happiness which hath no end." (Mormon 7:7; emphasis added)

The Doctrine of One God—A Testimony of the Book of Mormon

As the Prophet Joseph Smith is responsible for the doctrine of the godhead taught in the restored Church, he also is responsible for publishing the Book of Mormon. He surely would want these to be harmonious regarding this most fundamental doctrine. However, the preceding scriptural quotes seems to indicate differences about how many Gods there are. Even the published testimony of the three witnesses of the Book of Mormon concludes with, "And the honor be to the Father, and to the Son, and to the Holy Ghost, which is *one God.*"

Because the Book of Mormon itself testifies that it was written by Eastern, or oriental, writers (1 Nephi 1:2), evidence should exist that it indeed differed from Western thought. Joseph Smith never claimed to have *written* the Book of Mormon. On the contrary, he always said that it was written by prophets of the past. He did not write the book; he translated it (see title page of the Book of Mormon).

Over the years since its original publication, numerous changes in punctuation and spelling have been made. However, the doctrinal concept of *one* God has not been changed. These presumed difficulties within the Book of Mormon text are removed when Eastern usage of symbolism is applied. Remember, the Eastern manner of writing emphasizes a message, the details of which may not necessarily be true. However, that same culture's manner of expression attempts to give a message whose *total effect* is true and accurate. The statement that "these three are one" is a very Eastern message.

Abinadi and His Teachings

The incident for which the prophet Abinadi is best remembered occurs as he stands before the wicked King Noah and his priests. The priests, together with Noah, try to confuse and defeat Abinadi and, in so doing, ask him questions. When asked how

God will bear the sins of transgressors, Abinadi answers:

> Now Abinadi said unto them: I would that ye should understand that God himself shall come down among the children of men, and shall redeem his people.
>
> And because he dwelleth in flesh he shall be called the Son of God, and having subjected the flesh to the will of the Father, being the Father and the Son—
>
> The Father, because he was conceived by the power of God; and the Son, because of the flesh; thus becoming the Father and the Son—
>
> And they are one God, yea, the very Eternal Father of heaven and of earth." (Mosiah 15:1–4)

The plurality of the pronoun *them*, which is the antecedent to the term "one God," indicates that there are more Gods than one. Therefore, the *number* must not be the important element expressed in the statement. The message delivered to King Noah and his priests was that the gods they worshiped were not to be put in the same class as the Gods about whom Abinadi was teaching. Abinadi's Gods were exclusive; they were one! It is profound that the Gods of the Godhead be described in this manner. It is a testimony point that the Book of Mormon is Eastern in its nature and written by Eastern writers and therefore should be read with an Eastern mind and seen with an Eastern eye.

The Doctrine and Covenants Teaches One God

In the revelation that was to set the kingdom of God in order once again on the earth, the Prophet Joseph Smith received the following: "Which Father, Son, and Holy Ghost are one God, infinite and eternal, without end. Amen" (D&C 20:28).

Conclusion

By studying the various uses of the number one in scripture, we observe that the message is exclusion. We also note that the idea of exclusion applies most frequently to God because He is the most exclusive entity we know. We use this same idea in our own language when we want to tell somebody of his or her prominence in our affections. We might say to someone, "You are the one for me," or "You are my one and only." Competitive teams and fans often try to express the same kinds of ideas when they hold up one finger, indicating they are number one. They may do this even though they are still playing the game or if they have yet to play the other teams. When we apply this concept to the idea of God, it is powerful and promotes devotion, loyalty, and respect.

Returning to the symbolic power of the number one and revisiting the question of how many Gods rule in the heavens, perhaps we can appreciate more as to why God declares that the Father and the Son are one. By so saying, God is not attempting to tell us how many Gods there are. Numbers may not matter nearly as much for their literal value as they do for their symbolic value, what they say and how they express it.

To show that He and His Father are exclusive from all other gods, Jesus declares that they are one (see 3 Nephi 20:35; 28:10; D&C 50:43; 93:3). Of course they have unity. If they are exclusive, there must also be unity. Unity comes because there is no other option, not because of debate and investigation or because a consensus has been reached. There is simply only one idea or only one possibility. Oh, the beauty and power of the clear, doctrinally accurate, and distinct heavenly expression, "The father and I are one" (3 Nephi 11:27).

However, for many this declaration conjures up the question of how many gods are in the godhead. The debate and wrangling over this subject go far beyond being complicated. Nonetheless, we will see that prophets both ancient and modern have answered the question of how many gods there are with a proper Eastern answer—one!

2

The Number That Suggests Witnesses

When the number two is considered, we would do well to contrast it with what we know about the number one. As discussed, the basic concept behind the number one is exclusiveness. The basic thought behind the number two, on the other hand, is that now there is more than one. When we deal with number two, there is not just a single point of view—we must now recognize the point of view of another.

As an illustration, take a clean sheet of paper and draw a single dot with your pen or pencil. Now look at that dot; you will have unity in your opinions regarding it. You can't make comparisons with anything else. The same would be true if you had drawn a circle or a single image of any other kind.

But as soon as you add a second dot or image, everything changes. You can now make comparisons; you no longer have automatic, complete unity. There is now the possibility of differences. Your second mark may be larger or darker, or it may be different in shape and design. If there is no observable difference in these things, you may feel that they are the same. However, there has to be a difference if only in the position of the two marks on your paper. They cannot be on top of one another. There may be unity regarding many elements and observations of your two dots, but there is no total unity. There is the possibility of difference, whereas with only one dot or image, there is no possibility of difference.

When you add the second dot or image, you begin to experience the nature of the number two. Now let's transfer this concept to the realm of doctrine and ideas. When there is only one person or entity, no differences exist in ideas or doctrines that come from that person or entity. As soon as a second person or entity enters the picture, differences begin to occur.

It is much like the police interviewing a witness who observed a crime being committed from the east end of the block. The police can't find another witness and, therefore, have only one testimony. However, if they find a second witness who observed the same crime from the west end of the block, which was much closer to the scene of the crime, their report of the crime may change considerably. Even if this second witness also viewed the crime from the east end of the block, the possibility of difference in viewpoint would exist.

This is the fundamental idea behind the number two and its natural use. It sets itself apart from the number one by introducing significant contrast. Number one is exclusive; it is only one because there is no other. Compare that to the number two. Now there is another. The second can also be called on for its testimony, which may be different from the first; we acknowledge that the symbolic message of the number two is witness and testimony (see Fairbairn, *Teachers' and Students' Bible Encyclopedia,* 5: 37)

The Need for More than One Testimony

God has required that there be more than one witness for many things. Consider the following scriptures:

> At the mouth of two witnesses, or three witnesses, shall he that is worthy of death be put to death; but at the mouth of one witness he shall not be put to death. (Deuteronomy 17:6)

> One witness shall not rise up against a man for any iniquity, or for any sin, in any sin that he sinneth: at

the mouth of two witnesses, or at the mouth of three witnesses, shall the matter be established. (Deuteronomy 19:15)

But if he will not hear thee, then take with thee one or two more, that in the mouth of two or three witnesses every word may be established. (Matthew 18:16)

This is the third time I am coming to you. In the mouth of two or three witnesses shall every word be established. (2 Corinthians 13:1)

Because of the necessity of having two or more witnesses or testimonies for all the works and words of God and his people, the number two is associated with the idea of testimony or witnesses. God sets the pattern, and we find this pattern used consistently in the scriptures. Thus, when two objects, two peoples, two events, two entities, or two anything are mentioned, the idea of testimony and witness is the object of the recording. Illustrations of this kind of language are found throughout the scriptures.

Heaven and Earth As Witnesses

The two most dependable, consistent—and oldest—physical entities are called to the witness stand by God himself. Notice how God uses the two things most common to us all for this purpose:

"Out of *heaven* he made thee to hear his voice, that he might instruct thee: and upon *earth* he showed thee his great fire; and thou heardest his words out of the midst of the fire. . . . Give ear, O ye *heavens*, and I will speak; and hear, O *earth*, the words of my mouth (Deuteronomy 4:36; 32:1; emphasis added).

Heaven and earth are called upon to be witnesses to us of what God does in His role as father and God.

One of the most difficult times in God's dealing with His

disobedient and wayward children was when he brought them out of Egypt. It seems God wanted to be justified in the sight of all His children, then as well as thereafter. God knew there were two witnesses, sure witnesses of all He had done for those rebellious souls fresh from slavery in Egypt, so He called upon witnesses, two in number, and declared, "Hear, O *heavens*, and give ear, O *earth:* for the Lord hath spoken, I have nourished and brought up children, and they have rebelled against me" (Isaiah 1:2; emphasis added).

In the latter days, God called upon the same two witnesses on another vital matter. "Hear, O ye *heavens*, and give ear, O *earth*, and rejoice ye inhabitants thereof, for the Lord is God, and beside him there is no Savior" (D&C 76:1; emphasis added).

Two, Twice, and Double

When looking for the use of the number two as a symbol in the scriptures, its alternate forms must also be identified. When any of these are used, we have good reason to believe that they likewise suggest the idea of witnesses and testimony. For example, in Genesis we read how many times Joseph said that Pharaoh, king of Egypt, had received his dream from God: "And for that the dream was *doubled* unto Pharaoh *twice;* it is because the thing is established by God, and God will shortly bring it to pass" (Genesis 41:32; emphasis added).

Another example of this is found wherein God comforts Gideon and assures Gideon that He, God, will be with him as he leads Israel. God gives Gideon a second witness (Judges 6:36–40).

To Solomon, king of Israel, God also gave a message. The record tells us, "And the Lord was angry with Solomon, because his heart was turned from the Lord God of Israel, which had appeared unto him *twice*" (1 Kings 11:9; emphasis added).

Moses struck the rock *twice* (Numbers 20:11), from which water came, to give life to his wandering host.

Possibly the idea of two, or doubling (constituting a witness), was behind what Elisha looked for when he made his request of Elijah to "let a *double* portion of thy spirit be upon me" (2 Kings 2:9; emphasis added). His desire was to be as worthy, obedient, and faithful as Elijah. No wonder he wanted to be assured that he would have divine assistance. Surely he was not asking to be twice Elijah in anything. More likely, he wanted an assurance or testimony that he would be able to do some of what Elijah had accomplished.

The same logic should be applied to God's message as spoken by Isaiah and Jeremiah to the nation of Judah. Because of Judah's disobedience, they would be taken into captivity. Jeremiah wrote, "And first I will recompense their iniquity and their sin double; because they have defiled my land, they have filled mine inheritance with the carcases of their detestable and abominable things" (Jeremiah 16:18).

Judah's suffering was a double witness that they had been warned by a just God. He still loved the people but had to let justice fall, as evidenced by what Isaiah wrote: *"Comfort* ye, *comfort* ye my people, saith your God.

"Speak ye comfortably to Jerusalem, and cry unto her, that her warfare is accomplished, that her iniquity is pardoned: for she hath received of the Lord's hand *double* for all her sins (Isaiah 40:1–2; emphasis added).

Isaiah also wrote: "Behold, it is written before me: I will not keep silence, but will *recompense,* even *recompense* into their bosom, your *iniquities,* and *the iniquities of your fathers* together, saith the Lord, which have *burned incense* upon the mountains, and *blasphemed me* upon the hills: therefore will I measure their former work into their bosom" (Isaiah 65:6–7; emphasis added).

Notice the double emphasis on *recompense.* The people were to know that what they would experience was a testimony of their disobedience. Notice also that not only their own iniquities would bring this punishment upon them but also the iniquities of their fathers, which would be a second witness why God punished them. Their sins, though many, were categorized into two major transgressions. The whole verse is written and structured upon the message of the number two.

When reading the following verse, some wonder if God is going to destroy His people twice. However, a more meaningful interpretation may be that God's actions were a witness or testimony that what He says will be fulfilled: "Let them be confounded that persecute me, but let not me be confounded: let them be dismayed, but let not me be dismayed: bring upon them the day or evil, and destroy them with double destruction" (Jeremiah 17:18; also Jude 1:12).

Likewise when God blessed Job, the record says: "And the Lord turned the captivity of Job, when he prayed for his friends: also the Lord gave Job *twice* as much as he had before" (Job 42:10; emphasis added; also Revelation 18:6). Both warnings and blessings can follow more than one witness.

The Savior was most likely experiencing this same message of testimony against the disobedient of His day when He said, "Woe unto you, scribes and Pharisees, hypocrites! For ye compass sea and land to make one proselyte, and when he is made, ye make him *twofold* more the child of hell than yourselves" (Matthew 23:15; emphasis added).

Angels, the Ark, and the Tablets

God's language and the language of His prophets are more complex than a simple literal reading reveals. We often find a subtle message, a message more important than just the factual description, waiting to be experienced by the reader who considers the symbolic and figurative. When God gives messages, He often uses more than one angel (Genesis 32:1,2; Daniel 12:5). Two cherubim were placed over the ark that was to reside in the tabernacle and temple. This ark was called the Ark of the Covenant, but it was also the Ark of Testimony (Exodus 25:22). Thus, we see the reason for two cherubim.

We should give this same consideration to the telling of the giving and receiving of the Ten Commandments. For instance, why couldn't the entire Decalogue be placed on one tablet? That seems a logical question, until we consider the message God is trying to send in addition to the Ten Commandments written on the tablets. Size would not have been the reason for putting them on two tables. The reason was that God had spoken, and He wanted his commands to be obeyed.

"And he gave unto Moses, when he had made an end of communing with him upon Mount Sinai, *two tables of testimony*, tables of stone, written with the finger of God" (Exodus 31:18; emphasis added). God wanted this to be witnessed and verified. That was the message that came into the minds of anyone who heard that the Ten Commandments were engraved on *two* tablets of stone.

To Second and to Witness

Sometimes we don't remember that in our own time, under parliamentary procedures, we second a motion. We can now see even more of a reason for this when we consider the pattern of witnesses and testimony established by God. All ordinances ordained by God, such as baptism and marriage, require two witnesses. For "in the mouth of two or three witnesses shall every word be established" (2 Corinthians 13:1; D&C 6:28).

Countless thousands have gone forth two by two, witnessing to the world as missionaries. Some have likely felt that their partner provided some degree of comfort and companionship, no matter how small. But the concept of witnesses is far more than that. This mode of laboring is a testimony and a witness in and of itself. The Lord dictated that His disciples should go two by two (Luke 10:1).

In a similar manner, when he recorded his gospel, the Apostle John wrote in an unusual way about himself and Peter's brother, Andrew. He refers to himself in third person and doesn't identify Andrew until four verses later. But in those six verses he uses the word *two* to refer to himself and Andrew. Many feel that John is thus setting himself up as a witness and, of course, his gospel as his testimony (John 1:35–40). In these few verses near the beginning of his testimony, John gives the flavor for his entire gospel. It is to be a *witness*, and the use of the word *two* seems to play a part in his testimony from the start.

Noah and the Ark

When we read that Noah took certain creatures into the ark by twos, we should be thinking of the reasons that this might be so. The possibility of *it* being merely practical and simplistic is real. However, note the following reasons that God would give directions using the number two.

First, God was testifying that there is a difference between creatures being male and female. Second, God was noting a distinction between creatures being clean and unclean. Third, God was testifying that the creatures of the earth were being destroyed for a just reason. Fourth, God was testifying that He was saving each species in the salvaging work of Noah and the ark.

The concept of showing a difference or distinction between two things that are supposed to be totally separate appears in the law given to Moses and is best illustrated when a child is born. If the newborn is female, the mother is isolated or "unclean" for two weeks (Leviticus 12:15)—twice the period of isolation if the child is male (Leviticus 12:2).

Thus, God indicates in this most common and relative process that a fundamental difference exists between maleness and femaleness. The law constitutes both a witness and a testimony that there exists a distinction between the two genders. In other words, a child could not be born in Israel without drawing attention to the difference between male and female. This gender difference went beyond simply observing the physical differences of genitalia; from the very moment of birth, parents were to relate their own behavior to the gender of the child.

This gender difference, as applied to humankind, is amply

applied to every living creature that survived the great flood. Noah is commanded to take of every creature, male and female, two of every kind. God did not just offer passage on the ark for whatever animals could be gathered or attracted to safety. As in all things He does, God sends messages that teach and govern.

Two Testaments

We can find ample reasons that biblical scholars would divide the Old and New Testaments, including their era, historical settings, life before Christ, dividing life before Christ from life after His coming in the flesh. However, the most powerful reason can be seen in the divine design that there would be more than one written witness of God and His work, that God was who He was before He was born as well as when He came to earth in the flesh.

As with the Ten Commandments, written on two tablets of stone, the Bible, with its two testaments, the old and the new, witnesses of the mercy, love, and providence of God. The two testaments witness that God, our Heavenly Father, has not changed in His eternal plan for us. He promised in the Old Testament that He would one day send His son as the Redeemer. The New Testament is the record of His fulfilling that promise. Together, they serve as two witnesses of His work on our behalf.

Another Testament of Christ

A careful study of 2 Nephi 27–29 reveals how God feels about the conditions under which He knows His children will reject His testimony that will some day come forth in the Bible. He warns those who will say that they have received the words of the Jews (the Bible) in this way: "Wo be unto him that saith; We have received, and we need no more" (2 Nephi 28:27).

And then God continues. "Wherefore murmur ye, because that ye shall receive more of my word? Know ye not that the testimony of two nations is a witness unto you that I am God, that I remember one nation like unto another? Wherefore, I speak the same words unto one nation like unto another. And when the two nations shall run together the testimony of the two nations shall run together also" (2 Nephi 29:8).

Officially named *The Book of Mormon, Another Testament of Jesus Christ*, the Book of Mormon was to come forth in a day when the words of the Bible would be disbelieved by the Gentiles as well as the Jews (1 Nephi 13:20–40). It would be the testimony that would help believers and the condemning witness or those who would not respond to the word of God.

Jesus' Need for Witnesses

If anyone exists who is able to stand alone, it would be the one who created both heaven and earth. But Jesus responded to the Jews who were intent on taking His life that both He and His Father had work to do. Then Jesus said the following:

> I can of mine own self do nothing: as I hear, I judge: and my judgment is just; because I seek not mine own will, but the will of the Father which hath sent me.
>
> If I bear witness of myself, my witness is not true.
>
> There is another that beareth witness of me; and I know that the witness which he witnesseth of me is true.
>
> Ye sent unto John, and he bare witness unto the truth.
>
> But I receive not testimony from man: but these things I say, that ye might be saved.
>
> He was a burning and a shining light: and ye were willing for a season to rejoice in his light.
>
> But I have greater witness than that of John: for the works which the Father hath given me to finish, the same works that I do, bear witness of me, that the Father hath sent me. (John 5:30–36)

Those words of the Savior seem to confuse some readers. Why doesn't He simply state that His Father is His witness? He brings up the matter of Him being His own witness, as well as the idea of John coming before Him to witness of His Messianic role. However, if the powerful message of the number two is applied to Jesus' words, clarity comes and lightens the scene, painting it with the same colors as the dual scenes of Eden and Sinai.

The "True" Witness

The last concept centers on surety. Witnesses are always used unless God Himself chooses to be his own witness (Hebrews 6:13). He needs no other, for His view never lacks in truth. He sees all. "For he knoweth all things, and there is not anything, save he knows it" (2 Nephi 9:20).

Jehovah is called the true witness (Revelation 3:14), and appropriately so because of His divine attributes. Additionally, Jesus is the second member of the godhead. As He and His Father are one, He is His own witness. You might ask why Jesus would need a witness and why would He set Himself as a witness for Himself?

The answers to these questions are found within the message of the number two. Christ complies with the eternal law that all things would be witnessed by two or more. The message of two is for us. We should know that things operate by plan and design. God does not simply do things by whim and impulse. God's word is as a two-edged sword (Hebrews 4:12). The message of a sword having two edges can be dualistic. Yes, it cuts both ways. Further, it never cuts where it shouldn't but always cuts where it should. However, the message of a two-edged sword also declares that there are always witnesses to God's word. Yes, His word is sharp, and it cuts; but it is two-edged, and, therefore, is a sure testimony to us.

Conclusion and Comparison

In baptism we take upon ourselves the name of Christ. At first, this procedure seems to refer to a single incident. However, upon closer examination, we find that the whole ordinance is draped by the idea of two. We are not just baptized, we are reborn.

Jesus told Nicodemus that he must be born again. He further instructed that all men must experience that same process in order to enter the kingdom of heaven. The idea of being *reborn* suggests the idea of *two*. First we are born and then reborn. When speaking to Nicodemus, Jesus not only reminded Nicodemus of things he had already experienced, but He spoke of the process that would now be required of Nicodemus.

Jesus explained that Nicodemus must be reborn and included in that message the idea of the number two. Upon further examination, however, it is evident that there are *two* births in addition to the mortal birth. Jesus taught that there is a baptism of the water and a baptism of the spirit (John 3:5). The idea that this one process, the process of being reborn, would have the essence of the number two is provoking. However, knowing how often God speaks and commands with the idea of witnesses as His purpose helps understand the dualism that we can identify in His words.

We should always look for the message of witnesses whenever we read the number two. The same should apply whenever we read of two occurrences or read of something being repeated, restated, or doubled.

3

The Number That Denotes a Fullness

While observing how numbers are used in scripture, we note that the number three is often used to describe the godhead, presidencies, bishoprics, and structures. Stories are told with three characters, three visits, or three main elements. Events take place for three hours, three days, or three years. The number three is used prolifically when comparing its usage to the number of times most other numbers are used. Regarding its use, we read, "The number three seems early to have attracted attention as the number in which beginning, middle, and end are most distinctly marked, and to have been therefore regarded as symbolic of a complete and ordered whole" *(The International Standard Bible Encyclopedia,* 1946, 2161).

The description of being a complete and ordered whole suggests fullness and sufficiency. Events or descriptions that have a beginning, middle, and end have a sense of being complete. If something is complete, there isn't anything lacking and, therefore, it is self-sufficient.

This sense that nothing is lacking comes through in everyday phrases and idioms such as hook, line, and sinker; the sun, the moon, and the stars; lock, stock, and barrel; and three strikes and you're out. The traits and characteristics of the godhead match perfectly these symbolic elements of the number three. The godhead is complete, ordered, full, and sufficient. The godhead not only has three members but is thought of as complete in love, power, and dominion. There is no diminishing from one element to another. So also is the symbolism for the number three.

As a representation of these ideas, the number three emphasizes recorded events, such as the three prayers suggested in Psalms 55:17 for morning, mid-day, and evening prayer. The symbol also adds significance to the three feasts that were to be observed: the Feast of Tabernacles, the Feast of Dedication, and the Feast of Passover (Exodus 23:14; Deuteronomy 16:16). Some animals for sacrifice had to be three years old (see Genesis 15:9). Fruit was not to be harvested until three years after the tree was planted (Leviticus 19:23).

The Savior was presented three temptations in the wilderness (Matthew 4:1–11). He offered prayer three times in Gethsemane (Matthew 26:39–45), and he rose on the third day after His death (Acts 10:40). These events assure the reader that the Savior was fully tempted, that he fully suffered, and that what He went through was complete, ordered, and sufficient. The message comes through forcefully when we combine the recorded details of the event with the use of the symbolic number three. The supposition seems to be appropriate that God ordained the event to have the three elements, or that the writer structured the account to include the number of elements, so that those who became aware of the events would sense the significance of it all.

Other instances using the number three also occurred. The Apostle Peter denied three times that he knew Jesus or was associated with him (Matthew 26:34–35, 69–75). Also, the Savior gave a powerful charge to Peter to feed His flock (John 21: 15–17). This charge was given three times with a slight variation each time. There was nothing lacking in the Savior's message. Peter and the other apostles who were present understood it completely. They received the message, and they refocused their commitment. They returned to feeding the flock—a calling from which they never departed or waivered.

The Number Three, or the Idea of Volume

Multiplying the two dimensions of an area—the length times the width—produces the area's number of square cubits, feet, or yards. However, such a calculation produces no volume. It isn't until a third dimension is multiplied that volume comes into play. When the length is multiplied by the width, and then the sum by the height, we determine the capacity or fullness within. The resulting volume is called cubic.

If the dimensions of length, width, and height are all the same, the object is called a cube, which is a form of the number three. A cube truly suggests volume and fullness. Now the question arises: What message could come to the heart and mind of someone in ancient Israel who approached the temple to worship? If that person was aware that the sanctuary that represented the dwelling place of God was, by measurement, a cube, what effect would that have? It would be a powerful confirmation that God was full, complete, and sufficient. This could apply to His power, love, compassion, or to any other godly attributes. The description of the Holy of Holies of the temple was given as follows: "And the oracle in the forepart was twenty cubits in length, and twenty cubits in breadth, and twenty cubits in the height thereof: and he overlaid it with pure gold; and so covered the alter which was of cedar" (1 Kings 6:20).

Surely, here was a symbol that provides additional suggestions to the mind of the worshiper. The individual boards of the walls of the inner sanctuary were each to be overlaid with pure gold, suggesting ideas about the glory of God and the richness of His kingdom. Other elements that often help the worshiper are colors, odors, and dimensions. God had many of these symbols designed into the temple of ancient Israel. The worshiper could count and notice that the large laver on the backs of twelve oxen had three oxen facing east, three oxen facing west, as well as three oxen facing both north and south.

The water was used for cleansing the offerings. What an important message to associate with this function! The priest who washed at the laver was to be completely clean. Likewise, the individual who gave the offering could expect a total and complete purging. The offering was to be made fully, completely, and sufficiently. John the Revelator described the New Jerusalem with similar characteristics: "On the east three gates; on the north three gates; on the south three gates; and on the west three gates" (Revelation 21:13).

The gates, of course, will be entrances. However, not everyone will enter the city designated as the dwelling place of the righteous. Three gates suggest to anyone who approaches that in order to enter he or she must be sufficient in righteousness and complete and full in all the necessary criteria for entering.

In our own time, one can't observe the Salt Lake Temple without noticing the three main towers on the east and the three additional towers on the west. They are not considered as six towers but as three representing the Melchizedek Priesthood and three, slightly lower than those on the east, representing the Aaronic Priesthood (see Truman O. Angel, "The Salt Lake City Temple'" *Millennial Star* 36, no. 18 [5 May 1874]: 274–75).

A power comes to the mind of observers of such features. That same power is missed by the unknowing person who does not know or does not comprehend or recognize the ways in which God communicates to His children. The simple spires, three in number, which stand on top of or alongside chapels and other places of worship, emit the same message to all who observe and understand.

This does not take away from structures that have a single spire, which convey the message of number one. Limitless messages can be given and received through the use of symbols. The use of a symbol on one structure does not preclude the use of another symbol on some other structure. Architects, like writers of scripture, chose symbols to communicate ideas. Observers are moved when they can identify and apply the privileged message.

Three Visits

Acts records the struggle the Apostle Peter had with the gospel being accepted by the Gentiles as well as the Jews. As leader of the Quorum of the Twelve Apostles, Peter appropriately received the vision teaching that Gentiles were not unclean and, therefore, the message of salvation should be taken to them also. The vision given to Peter to teach this powerful concept was given thrice (Acts 10:16).

The story of Samuel being called as a young servant to God has in it this same emphasis of fullness and completeness, wherein the angel speaks or calls to the young boy Samuel three times (1 Samuel 3:3–14). Eli told Samuel that because of the three calls, he knew the message was from God. Therefore, if it happened again, Samuel should answer.

There should be no doubt as to the significance of the visits of the angel Moroni to the Prophet Joseph Smith. Joseph observed that the three visits of Moroni took most of the night (see Joseph Smith–History 1:30–47) Two additional appearances by Moroni occurred the following day, wherein Moroni rehearsed and instructed Joseph in the same manner he did during the night. However, the story is recounted and remembered for its significance of three visits during the night as opposed to the five total visits.

Visits for Three Days

Alma the Younger needed a full and complete turnaround in his life. He was going the wrong way, and the whole Church, including his father, knew it. The verses that highlight details of his story wherein an angel appeared to him are as follows:

> And it came to pass that I fell to the earth; and it was for the space of three days and three nights that I could not open my mouth, neither had I the use of my limbs. . . .
>
> And now, for three days and for three nights was I

> racked, even with the pains of a damned soul. . . .
>
> And it came to pass that I was three days and three nights in the most bitter pain and anguish of soul; and never, until I did cry out unto the Lord Jesus Christ for mercy, did I receive a remission of my sins. But behold, I did cry unto him and I did find peace to my soul. (Alma 36:10, 16; Alma 38:8)

The retelling or recording of this event by Alma, with its use of the number three as a detail, also strongly indicates that the message was sufficient to fully purge out of Alma's life the things that were wrong.

Today, we may want to communicate to someone that we have done something enough times that we are very comfortable with the process. So we say, "Oh, I've done that hundreds of times." When we say such a thing, rarely does anyone ever challenge it by saying; "Oh, have you counted the number of times? I know you haven't done it more than fifty times." No, we recognize that there was a more important message, a message that goes beyond the exact number that was stated, whether accurate or not. The number three places emphasis on the event and on the suggestion of the fullness or the completeness of the event, its principle and practice.

We should remember that the Apostle Paul, when converted on the road to Damascus, experienced three days without sight (Acts 9:9). He also went without nourishment for that same period. Paul was completely and fully misguided in his belief regarding the life and mission of Jesus. Paul was going about "breathing out threatenings and slaughter against the disciples of the Lord" (Acts 9:1). When he went to Ananias, as he was instructed to do, Ananias put his hands upon him, blessed him with the return of his sight, and also blessed him with the Holy Ghost. "And immediately there fell from his eyes as it had been scales: and he received sight forthwith, and arose, and was baptized" (Acts 9:18).

We might wonder whether the author is attempting to tell us

that Paul went seventy-two hours without food and sight as much as he was attempting to describe how fully and completely was the change Paul experienced. He was transformed from an unbeliever to completely knowing of the mission of Jesus, the Messiah. The number three can figuratively indicate such a transformation, one that is not just partial or unfinished.

In Gethsemane, Jesus left His disciples to be by Himself for prayer. After praying, He returned to His Apostles, only to find them asleep. He asked Peter if he could not watch with Him one hour, then the Savior went away again for prayer by Himself. A second time Christ returned, only to find the disciples asleep. He requested again that they watch with Him while He prayed. Finally, a third time Jesus returned from prayer only to find his faithful followers deep in slumber.

The contrast of the story seems to indicate how out of tune the disciples were to what Jesus was doing. He was performing His great atoning work, and they clearly didn't fully comprehend the importance. This event takes place at the end of an intense training session, which included the Passover meal, the institution of the sacrament, the anointing of Jesus with oil, the determination to betray Jesus by Judas, and the warning to Peter that he would deny Jesus three times that very night.

The contrast between what Jesus was doing and what was important to the disciples, even Peter, may well be the symbol of three. The number seems to indicate the complete and full intent of the Savior compared to the incomplete and lacking devotion of the disciples.

We might ask why Matthew, one of those who slept, would include this incident in his testimony (Matthew 26). Logically one would think that he would exclude it from his text and not reveal any personal failure on his part. However, the possibility exists that Matthew sought to help others who have found it difficult to comprehend what Jesus had done. Perhaps others can find hope in the fact that Matthew, and even Peter, slept. How full and complete was their inattentiveness? It was three. And Jesus forgave them, even telling them to "sleep on" (Matthew 26:45)!

He understands that men find it challenging to understand the work of Gods.

Another biblical event that could have an additional message suggested by the number three is the request made by Moses to Pharaoh, king of Egypt, to let the children of Israel go three days' journey to offer sacrifices (Exodus 3:18; 5:3; Numbers 15:9). The children of Israel needed to be out of the land where improper sacrifices were being offered so that they could offer an acceptable offering to God.

Question: How far was that?

Answer: Three days' journey, or of sufficient distance to be clear of the land of unacceptable sacrifices.

When the Pharaoh did not let the Israelites go, both he and his people were exposed to three days of darkness (Exodus 10:22). That should have been a sufficient message as to the power of Moses' God. Later, the scriptures tell us, the children of Israel wandered in the wilderness without water for three days (Exodus 15:22).

If the record tries to be exact and specific for the entire group, it seems likely that some went longer than three days without water while others probably went without water less than that. However, this symbol communicates that the children of Israel had gone such a great distance that they were fully in need of divine help. Their need for water was complete and absolute.

In the Book of Mormon, when Nephi and Lehi are in prison, the voice of God is heard three times (Helaman 5:21–33). The walls then tumble, and the two are delivered. When the Savior appears to the Nephites in the land Bountiful, He is announced by the Father, and only the third time is His voice heard (3 Nephi 11:1-7). The people are certain who is speaking and they also know who is being announced.

Sometimes we may notice instructions that have three elements such as, "*Search* diligently, *pray* always, and *be believing*" (D&C 90:24; emphasis added). Such use of the number three, or the listing of three elements, may be simply coincidence. However, the message of the number three as a symbol may well be intended to enhance and amplify the event or the principles being considered.

The event in which the Savior tells Peter to feed His flock also includes the Savior asking three times if Peter loves Him (see John 21:15–17). In these verses, the number three does not appear, though it does in the preceding verse (14). The possible emphasis of the number three may well be considered in light of the great effort this apostle makes to be complete, full, and sufficient in his testimony of the Messiah.

David and Jonathan

We can look at the story of David and Jonathan in a similar way. Jonathan is the princely son to King Saul. However, God has rejected Saul for disobedience, and therefore, his son Jonathan will have no throne to inherit. Meanwhile, God has anointed David to be the next king. But the interesting thing is that David and Jonathan are best friends, very close and dependent on one another.

After an emotional event wherein Jonathan, by coded message, communicates to David that Saul, his father, intends to kill David, David bids farewell to Jonathan and tries to show his feelings and devotion to his friend, even though Jonathan is not to be king. David "fell on his face to the ground, and bowed himself three times: and they kissed one another, and wept one with another" (1 Samuel 20:41).

What a message! What better way could David communicate to his friend the emotions he felt? He was trying to show how fully and completely he felt, how humbled he was that Jonathan had not betrayed him, and how grateful he was that Jonathan had honored the wishes of God.

Jonah and Three

Jonah was called to preach to Nineveh, but because of fear he turned away from his mission. For three days he was caught in this terrible turmoil. The idea that he was fully caught and completely in need of divine intervention in his life seems more important than how long he was held captive "in the belly of the fish" (Jonah 1–2).

Almost any amount of time in such a predicament would destructive. But the reader of the account can sense how desperate Jonah was, in addition to how sufficient was the help he received, if the symbolic message of the number three is applied.

Nephi, Isaiah, and Jacob

Nephi recorded that he had seen the Lord. He indicated that he was not alone in this significant event to which he wanted to testify. Just before quoting Isaiah, he wrote:

> And now I, Nephi, write more of the words of Isaiah, for my soul delighteth in his words. For I will liken his words unto my people, and I will send them forth unto all my children, for he verily saw my Redeemer, even as I have seen him.
>
> And my brother, Jacob, also has seen him as I have seen him; wherefore, I will send their words forth unto my children to prove unto them that my words are true. Wherefore, by the words of three, God hath said, I will establish my word. Nevertheless, God sendeth more witnesses, and he proveth all his words. (2 Nephi 11:2–3)

Two or Three Witnesses?

When we consider the numerous scriptural passages that discuss how many witnesses the Lord requires, there seems to be some confusion. We might think that God should not be confused or unclear when giving His instructions to His people. We, not God, should be the ones with some uncertainty. Why would God provide an option, the option of having two *or* three? And, if God knows how many witnesses are best, why does He say "two or three"? Why not a definite number?

Some of the verses of scripture that use both two and three for the number of required witnesses include the following:

> At the mouth of *two* witnesses, or *three* witnesses, shall he that is worthy of death be put to death; but at the mouth of one witness he shall not be put to death. (Deuteronomy 17:6; emphasis added)

> One witness shall not rise up against a man for any iniquity, or for any sin, in any sin that he sinneth: at the mouth of *two* witnesses, or at the mouth of *three* witnesses, shall the matter be established. (Deuteronomy 19:15; emphasis added)

> But if he will not hear thee, then take with thee one or *two* more, that in the mouth of *two* or *three* witnesses every word may be established. (Matthew 18:16; emphasis added)

> This is the third time I am coming to you. In the mouth of *two* or *three* witnesses shall every word be established. (2 Corinthians 13:1; emphasis added)

> Against an elder receive not an accusation, but before *two* or *three* witnesses. (1 Timothy 5:19; emphasis added)

> He that despised Moses' law died without mercy under *two* or *three* witnesses. (Hebrews 10:28; emphasis added)

> And now, behold, I give unto you, and also unto
> my servant Joseph, the keys of this gift, which shall
> bring to light this ministry; and in the mouth of *two* or
> *three* witnesses shall every word be established. (D&C
> 6:28; emphasis added)

Rather than suspect God of indecision, let us look at the symbolism portrayed by each of the numbers mentioned. As discussed previously, the number two symbolizes more than one, that there is an additional witness. Use of the number two suggests that there is more than just one point of view, more than one testimony, that another viewpoint exists so that both may testify and verify.

Add to that thought the message of the number three and the concept appears that the testimony is full and complete. Nothing else is needed; it is sufficient. In other words, we are guided by the voice of one. Two witnesses provide us assurance upon which we may move. But with three witnesses, we have no reason not to move ahead fully justified. Two witnesses are sufficient. Three witnesses are even more desirable. Therefore, two or three.

The historical account of the coming forth of the Book of Mormon reveals that Joseph Smith learned at one point that there would be three who would testify concerning the plates. In addition, these three would testify that they had not only seen the plates but that they had seen the messenger, Moroni, who had delivered the plates to Joseph.

This understanding that there were to be three witnesses of this work, the Book of Mormon, was talked about early in the record itself (see 2 Nephi 27:2; Ether 5:2–4). As two witnesses would have been sufficient to make the case, what message was God giving when He directed that there would be three? The answer has been given before—to indicate completeness.

How many bear record in heaven and on earth? Consider the following verses: "For there are *three* that bear record in heaven, the *Father*, the *Word*, and the *Holy Ghost*: and these *three are one*.

"And there are three that bear witness in earth, the *Spirit*, and the *water*, and the *blood*: and these three agree in *one*" (1 John 5:7–8; emphasis added).

Turning this question of how many witnesses are required from confusion into the positive suggestion of infallible truth adds clarity to what has been written in the scriptures concerning witnesses.

Parable of the Wicked Husbandmen

Luke, as well as Matthew and Mark, includes the parable of a certain man who planted a vineyard, let it out to husbandmen, and then went into a far country for a long time (Luke 20:9–18; Matthew 21:33–40; Mark 12:1–9). The owner of the vineyard sent a servant to receive fruit or rent from the husbandmen. However, the husbandmen beat the servant and sent him away with nothing. The owner sent a second servant, who was likewise beaten, as well as a third, who was mistreated and cast out.

The story, though possibly real, seems to be used by the Savior in order to foretell a future event of utmost significance. Why did He tell the story with three servants who were rejected? The answer is that it suggests that the owner had completely and sufficiently made requests for justified compliance by the husbandmen. Since the husbandmen had rejected and abused all three servants, the symbolism of the number three suggests that the abuse and rejection were complete and sufficient for the landowner to exact proper payment from the wicked husbandmen.

What a humbling concept! When the idea of completeness and fullness is combined with the powerful message of wicked husbandmen, this story completely illustrates the ingratitude and abuse shown by the husbandmen. The reader should also not miss the symbolism of the parable, wherein the Savior is represented by the son, whom the owner of the vineyard finally sends to collect his just dues. Do we, like the wicked husbandmen, do to the son what was done in the parable?

Trilogies and Triads

The use of three servants in the story resembles stories of our own day. When someone tells you a funny story, it may begin with a person who says or does something absurd. A second person is next introduced, often on the other side of the spectrum of absurdity. And if you have not listened well to the first two elements, you may still be able to catch the jest and have a good laugh because a third person generally completes the absurdity.

You may also find it humorous because the story covers the subject completely or it is completely absurd. When the person who tells the story is finished, you will likely continue your conversation, not even aware of the dynamics of the number three. However, this very number set the scene and provided the elements that made you laugh. It may even have helped you identify elements in your own life to help you understand human nature a little better.

This pattern of completeness or fullness is also found in poetic triads and musical triads. It appears at the heart of trilogies written by the likes of C. S. Lewis and J. R. R. Tolkien. This idea of fullness is suggested in the trilogy by Bruce C. Hafen, *The Believing Heart*, *The Broken Heart*, and *The Becoming Heart*.

This accepted method of presenting an idea or concept by displaying three illustrations of it seems so natural. Thus, whenever the message of the number three is applied to a particular phenomenon, one begins to feel a sense about the subject that is full or complete. The urgency and message of the subject, in other words, is not simple and benign. Instead it has magnitude and deserves consideration because it comprehends things and events to their fullest extent.

Other Familiar Threes

The Apostle Paul indicates in his epistle to the Corinthians that if we do not have three certain things, we are nothing (1 Corinthians 13:2). Careful reading of the chapter demonstrates how, in his Eastern manner, he emphasizes one of the three—charity. The other two elements—*faith* and *hope*—are not even mentioned until the last verse, which simply states, "And now abideth faith, hope, charity, these three; but the greatest of these is charity" (1 Corinthians 13:13).

Paul gives a detailed analysis of charity, but he does not give a single definition or illustration of faith or hope. So why does he even mention the other two? The answer comes in the manner of Paul's writing and the pattern of the writing of others of his time and culture.

Paul uses the symbol three to teach the principles it represents: fullness, sufficiency, and completeness. If a person has faith in addition to hope and charity, then that person will be complete. He or she will be sufficiently empowered to deal with any challenge.

The apostle John uses the same symbolic pattern but with three descriptive names that refer to Jesus. In his declaration to the seven churches, he refers to Jesus as "him which is, and which was, and which is to come" (Revelation 1:4).

The manner of speech of other scriptural verses seems similarly designed to give emphasis to a message. Isaiah wrote, "And one cried unto another, and said, Holy, holy, holy, is the Lord of hosts: the whole earth is full of his glory" (Isaiah 6:3). The message? The earth is full (three) of His glory. He is completely holy. He lacks nothing. He is totally sufficient. The same message can be understood in such triads as the *spirit*, the *water*, and the *blood* (1 John 5:8), and "I am the *way*, the *truth*, and the *life*" (John 14:6).

Under the Law of Moses, three cities were appointed as places of refuge, where individuals needing mercy and understanding could go (Deuteronomy 19:2). In another instance, blood from a sacrifice was to be placed upon the tip of the *right ear*, upon the *thumb* of the right hand, and upon the *great toe* of the right foot of Aaron (Leviticus 8:24). The blood represented the blood of the promised Savior and the effect His power would have upon those represented by Aaron. This effect was to be nothing short of full, complete, and sufficient. Other threes within the Law of Moses can be identified to show the same rationale.

The Woes

The prophet Samuel the Lamanite, as well as many other prophets, warned people using a single wo. "Yea, *Wo* unto this people, because of this time which has arrived, that ye do cast out the prophets, and do mock them, and cast stones at them, and do slay them, and do all manner of iniquity unto them, even as they did of old time" (Helaman 13:24; emphasis added).

King Benjamin warned his people using two *woes*: "But *wo, wo* unto him who knoweth that he rebelleth against God! For salvation cometh to none such except it be through repentance and faith on the Lord Jesus Christ" (Mosiah 3:12; emphasis added).

The Book of Mormon, Pearl of Great Price, and Doctrine and Covenants all contain numerous uses of the word *wo*, which is best defined as calamity and imminent punishment. Most of these warnings are spoken by Jehovah, while others are uttered by God the Father and various prophets. But on one occasion, when incredible destructions had occurred to unrepentant peoples in numerous cities, Jesus Christ speaks to those who have been spared, explaining why so many have been sent to their death:

"*Wo, wo, wo* unto this people; *wo* unto the inhabitants of the whole earth except they shall repent; for the devil laugheth, and his angels rejoice, because of the slain of the fair sons and daughters of my people; and it is because of their iniquity and abominations that they are fallen" (3 Nephi 9:2; emphasis added).

The Savior's imperative manner of speaking to His people indicates that they had been fully and completely warned. The use of the three woes represents that message. Likewise King Benjamin's warning, wherein he uses two woes, indicates that there were witnesses who had testified as a warning against those who were rebelling against God. His use of two woes gives his message as an added emphasis.

Bishoprics and Presidencies

A bishop serving with two counselors constitutes a bishopric. When we apply the symbolism of the number three as a help in understanding the work performed by bishoprics, we observe that strength and power can come to the mind and heart through their combined efforts. The thousands who have served in bishoprics were reassured that they were not serving alone. Knowing that God ordained that there are to be three members in a bishopric should be a message that three individuals thus called are fully sufficient for the work assigned. The three can do what is needed, completely and in proper order.

Those who look at this presiding quorum in a ward, sometimes with doubt as to their abilities and capabilities, should have an increase of faith in their bishopric as they consider the symbolism associated with the number three.

Presidencies also function within the framework of three—a president and two counselors. Of the presidency of the Church, the Lord said, "Of the Melchizedek Priesthood, three Presiding High Priests, chosen by the body, appointed and ordained to that office, and upheld by the confidence, faith, and prayer of the church, form a quorum of the Presidency of the Church" (D&C 107:22).

When a member of the Church considers the phrase "three Presiding High Priests," a surge of faith and devotion should be felt in the soul because of the message of fullness, completeness, and sufficiency suggested by the number three. Presidencies of all other quorums and auxiliaries deserve the same feelings because all presidencies have three members.

The number three appears prominent even though the Lord directs that presidencies and bishoprics can call a secretary or clerk. When Church members are asked how many individuals make up a bishopric, the answer is generally four or five; they are uncertain whether the executive secretary and ward clerk are included. However, the Lord's definition of a bishopric is three: a bishop and two counselors.

Some contend that clerks and secretaries should be considered a part of those presidencies because they often do as much or more work than the presiding members. This points well to the issue. It seems once again that the Lord is probably more interested in telling us how members of the bishopric are to act and how we are to feel about their service. This is more important than how many serve in a bishopric or presidency. Once again, the symbolism of the number teaches us, if we are aware what the figure represents.

In Heaven

We believe that because God is just we will all receive rewards that fully compensate us for everything, both good or evil, that we have done. Our reward will be complete. Nothing will be left out, and things will be thorough and just. The reward we inherit will be entirely suitable for us.

How does God communicate this to us? He has told us that there are three heavens or degrees of life beyond death and judgment. He has named and numbered them (1 Corinthians 15:40–41; D&C 76:70, 71, 81, 91, 92). The Apostle Paul was caught up to the "*Third* heaven" (2 Corinthians 12:2; emphasis added). This third heaven is also called or named the celestial kingdom. The other two are known as the terrestrial and telestial.

We are given another truth about what God has planned for His faithful in a description of the highest of these kingdoms, the celestial. God says, "In the celestial glory there are *three* heavens or degrees" (D&C 131:1; emphasis added). Thus, the reward God has planned for the most faithful is three multiplied by three—a more complete fullness than we can even imagine.

Third Part and One Third

The scriptural use of the word *third*, coupled with other words or factors, can leave us with questions. Does the word indicate position, as in "You are third?" Is the word used to indicate an amount, as in one third? And is one third the same as third part?

One third generally assess an amount that is one of three equal parts of a whole. That may be much different from a *third part*. Believing that these two terms mean the same thing could be misleading. For example, John the Revelator wrote: "And his tail drew the third part of the stars of heaven, and did cast them to the earth" (Revelation 12:4).

Many readers of this verse have identified it as an indicator of how many followed Lucifer in our premortal existence. From such a conclusion, one might make deductions that lead to troublesome results. Some have tried to determine approximately how many births have occurred since Adam and Eve and then divide that number in half. The resulting number, by deduction, would then be the number of unembodied spirits working to tempt and mislead us here in mortality. This large number has been used to alarm those trying to avoid evil influences.

However, John's use of the term *third part* may well need another interpretation. Using the figurative or symbolic ideas for the number three, or third, could his message have been that those who were drawn away by the tail of the beast constituted a fullness? Further, could his statement also indicate that none escaped a proper consequence or judgment for their rebellion, that their damnation was complete? As not all were drawn away, John used the symbolic third part, which could be far different from a literal one third.

Some may ask for an indicator as to whether this or other numbers should be literal or figurative. One of the first things that should be noted is all of the other figurative terms that accompany the third part of John's book. Consider the surrounding verses and ask how many literal usages of numbers appear as opposed to figurative ones:

> And there appeared a great wonder in heaven; a
> woman clothed with the sun, and the moon under her

feet, and upon her head a crown of twelve stars:

And she being with child cried, travailing in birth, and pained to be delivered.

And there appeared another wonder in heaven; and behold a great red dragon, having seven heads and ten horns, and seven crowns upon his heads.

And his tail drew the third part of the stars of heaven, and did cast them to the earth: and the dragon stood before the woman which was ready to be delivered, for to devour her child as soon as it was born. (Revelation 12:1–4)

John clearly writes with a figurative hand. It is difficult to find anything in these verses that is literal. He is painting a picture that stirs readers to action and awareness. His use of numbers in these verses reinforces that goal. The choice should be to consider his phrase as idiomatic and figurative; very little in the entire book written by John is literal. It is esoteric and full to the brim with symbols.

Three Days in the Tomb

Of utmost significance concerning the number three is a lack of clarity concerning the length of time our Lord's body lay in the tomb prior to His resurrection. Trying to deduct time measured by days or hours makes it difficult to reconcile the chronology with what scripture says of the event. Knowing that Jesus' body was taken down from the cross just prior to the beginning of the Sabbath (Friday at sundown) and placed in the tomb provides a beginning point for measuring. The end count accepted by most Christians is the early morning of Sunday, the first day of the week. That would total only parts of three days, not three whole days. Instead of being 72 hours (three days), the total time would be nearer 42 hours. However, forty-two hours does not agree with the three days spoken of in the following scriptures:

And he began to teach them, that the Son of man

must suffer many things, and be rejected of the elders, and of the chief priests, and scribes, and be killed, and after three days rise again. (Mark 8:31, see also Matthew 27:63)

Behold, they will crucify him; and after he is laid in a sepulcher for the space of three days he shall rise from the dead, with healing in his wings; and all those who shall believe on his name shall be saved in the kingdom of God. Wherefore, my soul delighteth to prophesy concerning him, for I have seen his day, and my heart doth magnify his holy name. (2 Nephi 25:13)

If the reader uses the symbolism of the number three and reads with the mind of an Easterner, not looking for an account accurate and literal in every detail as much as for one whose total effect is true, then these passages offer the message that our Lord did fully and completely what was necessary to complete His atoning sacrifice. He entered the tomb and came forth on His own. This is the message of three. Just as Jonah was delivered from the belly of the whale, Jesus would fully overcome the tomb:. "For as Jonas was three days and three nights in the whale's belly; so shall the Son of Man be three days and three nights in the heart of the earth" (Matthew 12:40).

In a similar way, Jesus spoke of taking up His body again. His critics supposed He was speaking of the physical temple, but "Jesus answered and said unto them, Destroy this temple, and in three days I will raise it up" (John 2:19).

We also have a further record of Him saying, "I will destroy this temple that is made with hands, and within three days I will build another made without hands" (Mark 14:58).

Our Savior did not need three days to rebuild either His body or the temple. He could do that with no time constraints whatever. But the message was not about the length of time as much as it was about what was to be accomplished and the significance of it.

Conclusion

The evidence relative to the symbolic nature of the number three is like a mountain. Much of the time it isn't noticed and is just felt to be part of the landscape. But if assessed, it is enormous and stands every day to be observed, examined, and admired. Triads, or statements that contain three elements that sum up the whole of a matter, suggest completeness, fullness, and sufficiency. Triads would include a beginning, a middle, and an end.

The number three includes the length, width, and depth. The idea of the number three is in the sun, moon, and stars (Joel 3:15). The sum of all human ability is expressed by the three elements of thought, word, and deed. Everything under the earth, upon the earth, as well as in the heavens above falls within the meaning of the number three. All things are present in "things as they are, and as they were, and as they are to come" (D&C 93:24). The past, present, and future are manifest in the scriptural phrase, "yesterday, today and forever," (D&C 20:12; Hebrews 13:8), and in statements calling upon wind, earthquake, and fire (1 Kings 19:11–12), as well as water, blood, and spirit (Moses 6:59–60; 1 John 5:8).

Isaiah described God in the following manner: "One cried unto another, and said, Holy, holy, holy, is the Lord of hosts: the whole earth is full of his glory" (Isaiah 6:3).

John likewise used the word *holy* three times in another triad: "Holy, holy, holy, Lord God Almighty, which *was*, and *is*, and *is to come*" (Revelation 4:8; emphasis added).

In the godhead, there are three, and they are one (1 John 5:7). Oh, the power of that scriptural declaration! The number three suggests that these members of the godhead are the essence of fullness, lacking nothing. They are one in that they are exclusive of all other gods or influences. They are united, and no other thing exists that can be compared to them.

Would any believer want the godhead any other way? The literal words of that statement have confused so many. However, the messages that come from the statement, when there is understanding of the symbolic nature of the numbers used, can and should be profound and moving.

While searching for statements that declare and reflect the essence of the number three, the testimony and revelation given on the day the Church was organized in the latter days come to mind. A single verse denotes the symbolic number one, just as a triadic expression suggests the number three. This verse states, "Which Father, Son, and Holy Ghost are one God, *infinite* and *eternal*, without *end*. Amen" (D&C 20:28; emphasis added).

4

The Number That Reflects Universality

Use of the number four in the scriptures seems to be largely confined to an association with the earth and its elements. Richard D. Draper writes that the number four is a symbol for geographic totality (*Opening the Seven Seals*, 94).

Noticed early when examining the number four are the four points of the compass: north, south, east, and west. Clear and distinct are the four seasons of the earth and four phases of the moon. We cannot do any physical labor at all without considering the four dimensions of length, width, height, and time. The day of creation when these things came into being was the fourth day (Genesis 1:14–19). These coordinates of the earth and phases of the heavens denote all locations and seasons man may encounter, no matter where he goes.

Genesis records that out of Eden went a river that had four heads or branches. The river seems to be described as watering the whole of the known world (Genesis 2:10–14). The "four winds from the four corners of heaven" are mentioned (Jeremiah 49:36), as well as the four corners of the earth (see Isaiah 11:12). The suggestion of geographic totality can be felt by these verses.

The Message of Totality—Israelite and Gentile

Four beasts sum up the Gentile empires, with their sovereignty over all the earth (Revelation 4:6). They watch over the Gentile nations. However, John also saw "another angel fly in the midst of heaven, having the everlasting gospel to preach unto them that dwell on the earth" (Revelation 14:6). This angel would restore the gospel so that it could be proclaimed to the Gentile nations of the earth. Because of Israel's scattering to all parts of the earth, these nations would have in them the assimilated blood of Israel to whom the gospel must be preached (2 Nephi 10:8).

Notice, by coincidence or symbolic pattern, how the gospel is to be taken to every (1) nation, (2) kindred, (3) tongue, and (4) people (Revelation 14:6). John varies his labels in Revelation 5:9 to (1) kindred, (2) tongue, (3) people, and (4) nation. But he did not change the number of classes. The pattern of four is there for the reader to understand concerning to whom the gospel is to be taken. It is to go to everyone!

Notice also the use of the number four in the following scriptures that deal with proclaiming the gospel to everyone: "And he shall send his angels with a great sound of a trumpet, and they shall gather together his elect from the *four winds*, from one end of heaven to the other" (Matthew 24:31; emphasis added). And again, "Then shall he send his angels, and shall gather together his elect from the *four winds*, from the uttermost part of the earth to the uttermost part of heaven" (Mark 13:27; emphasis added).

Concerning God's people, Israel who had been scattered throughout the nations of the earth, we read: "And it shall come to pass that they shall be gathered in from their long dispersion, from the isles of the sea, and from the *four parts* of the earth; and the nations of the Gentiles shall be great in the eyes of me, saith God, in carrying them forth to the lands of their inheritance" (2 Nephi 10:8; emphasis added).

Another example is found in 2 Nephi: "And he shall set up an ensign for the nations, and shall assemble the outcasts of Israel, and gather together the dispersed of Judah from the *four corners* of the earth" (2 Nephi 21:12; emphasis added; compare Isaiah 11:12).

To those who were given the keys of missionary work in the last days, who would be ordained apostles, the following is recorded: "After this vision closed, the heavens were again opened to us; and Moses appeared before us, and committed unto us the keys of the gathering of Israel from the *four parts* of the earth, and the leading of the ten tribes from the land of the north" (D&C 110:11; emphasis added).

And we read this: "This proclamation shall be made to all the kings of the world, to the *four corners* thereof, to the honorable president-elect, and the high-minded governors of the nation in which you live, and to all the nations of the earth scattered abroad" (D&C 124:3; emphasis added).

And again, "Which Twelve hold the keys to open up the authority of my kingdom upon the *four corners* of the earth, and after that to send my word to every creature" (D&C 124:128; emphasis added).

Apostles have the ordained assignment of being witnesses of God to the entire world, not just to those who believe them. The use of the number four is an emphasis of that divine commission that the apostles can't sidestep.

The Apostle Peter and His Vision

When the Apostle Peter was faced with the pressing question of whether the gospel should be taken to the Gentiles as well as to the Jews, he received a vision from God. He was shown a great sheet that contained animals of every kind, both clean and unclean. He was commanded to eat of every kind. From this vision, he understood the message that to God all His children were clean and worthy to receive the gospel. This universality was taught in one descriptive element of the vision (watch for the number four): "And [he] saw heaven opened, and a certain vessel descending unto him, as it had been a great sheet knit at the four corners, and let down to the earth" (Acts 10:11).

Peter retold this story using the same description. He said, "I was in the city of Joppa praying: and in a trance I saw a vision, A certain vessel descend, as it had been a great sheet, let down from heaven by four corners; and it came even to me" (Acts 11:5).

The Round Earth Has Corners

It is unusual to think of the globe we call earth as having corners. But when applying the symbolic meaning of the number four to the earth and its waters, skies, and lands, one begins to see that it is a message of totality, of everyone and everything. No one will be left out. Things that are to happen in the earth are mentioned in fours. This is exemplified in the four horsemen of Revelation 6. Each of the four represents things that are to happen on the earth during its history. The number four suggests that those will affect all.

Four Gospels

The number of gospels contained in the Bible—the accounts of the Savior's life and mission—can also be considered. Some have unknowingly supposed that in the Bible we have all of the written accounts. Others may feel that it is simply coincidence that four gospels were selected for inclusion in the sacred collection. Luke, whom most believe wrote his account after the others had recorded theirs, wrote to an associate, "Forasmuch as many have taken in hand to set forth in order a declaration of those things which are most surely believed among us . . . " (Luke 1:1). Note the words "as many have taken in hand." In addition to the four gospels we have in the New Testament, Coptic texts have come forth that contain the gospels of Thomas and Philip, as well as the Gospel of Truth.

Since many possessed written accounts of the Messiah and

His ministry, we wonder if it is more than simply coincidence that not all of the accounts were included in the Bible. Is there significance in the number of records chosen?

There exist symbolic reasons for the number of books contained in the Bible, as well as how many books are included in each of the Old and New Testaments. Some scholars suggest that the four testimonies or gospels were selected to declare that the message of this universal book was to go into all four parts of the earth—to every nation, kindred, tongue, and people.

Richard Draper finds this same symbolism regarding the judgments of God coming upon everyone, not just those of the apostle John's world. Draper's conclusion springs out of John the Revelator's use of the distance of 1600 furlongs in Revelation 14:20, which is the square of the number four, multiplied by the number ten squared. He states, "Taken together, the number suggests that God's judgment actually involves all John's world, not just those who are around Jerusalem, and that all those who belong to that portion outside the protecting power of God will be directly affected" (*Opening the Seven Seals*, 164).

The Feeding of the Thousands

The scriptures contain two accounts wherein the Savior feeds large numbers of people with small amounts of available food. The number of people fed on both occasions is noted in the accounts; both number in the thousands, one being four thousand and the other five thousand. It is certainly possible that the count on each occasion was exactly four thousand and five thousand. However, for all the symbolic reasons given previously, we have good reason to believe that the writer is telling us something more important than the exact number fed. Might the writer be trying to tell *who* was fed as well as how many?

The feeding of the four thousand (see Matthew 15:32–39) may well have been a feeding of a group of Gentiles or a group that had Gentiles in it as well as Jews. The number recorded, therefore, could possibly be as much an indicator of who was taught and fed as it was how many.

Four Beasts and Four Angels

Joseph Smith asked for help in understanding the elements described in Revelation 6:4. He asked, "What are we to understand by the four beasts, spoken of in the same verse?" The answer: "They are figurative expressions, used by the Revelator, John, in describing heaven, the paradise of God, the happiness of man, and of beasts, and of creeping things, and of the fowls of the air; that which is spiritual being in the likeness of that which is temporal; and that which is temporal in the likeness of that which is spiritual; the spirit of man in the likeness of his person, as also the spirit of the beasts, and every other creature which God has created" (D&C 77:2).

Joseph then asked, "Are the four beasts limited to individual beasts, or do they represent classes or orders?" He received this answer: "They are limited to four individual beasts, which were shown to John, to represent the glory of the classes of beings in their destined order or sphere of creation, in the enjoyment of their eternal felicity" (D&C 77:3).

Joseph Smith also asked, "What are we to understand by the four angels, spoken of in the 7th chapter and 1st verse of Revelations?"

He was answered, "We are to understand that they are four angels sent forth from God, to whom is given power over the four parts of the earth, to save life and to destroy; these are they who have the everlasting gospel to commit to every nation, kindred, tongue, and people; having power to shut up the heavens, to seal up unto life, or to cast down to the regions of darkness" (D&C 77:8).

Knowing the symbolic message of the number four surely enhances the declarations of the gospel being taken to every (1) nation, (2) kindred, (3) tongue, and (4) people (D&C 42:58). The gospel is to be taken to everyone; none will escape the message that is to visit every clime.

Sore Judgments

Ezekiel foretells the judgments of God that will come upon the disobedient of his people. It becomes apparent that these judgments would be without exception and be inclusive of all who turn from God to sin, Ezekiel states, "For thus saith the Lord, God; How much more when I send my four sore judgments upon Jerusalem, the sword, and the famine, and the noisome beast, and the pestilence, to cut off from it man and beast?" (Ezekiel 14:21) Note the four judgments: (1) the sword, (2) the famine, (3) the noisome beast, and (4) the pestilence. These are listed in addition to the use of the number four itself.

A similar pattern is observed in John's vision of the pale horse. He wrote, "And I looked, and behold a pale horse: and his name that sat on him was Death, and Hell followed with him. And power was given unto them over the fourth part of the earth, to kill with sword, and with hunger, and with death, and with the beasts of the earth" (Revelation 6:8).

The message of this event may be interpreted by some that these judgments would be over only one-fourth of the earth. However, in light of the symbolic nature of the number four, or fourth, the message coming from John is that judgment would be over the entire earth, universally and totally; there will be no exceptions. And the judgments listed are again four in number, with some difference from those mentioned by Ezekiel: (1) sword, (2) hunger, (3) death, and (4) beasts of the earth.

Servants Need to Be Totally Committed

Beyond simply considering the number four as used to define the nations and the boundaries of heaven and earth, the number four can also be observed in dealing with the inward or spiritual, the boundaries of the soul. In a revelation to Joseph Smith Sr., the Lord declares that he, Joseph Sr., was called to the work. However, the Lord also seems to open the invitation to all, for He says, "If ye have desires to serve God, ye are called to the work" (D&C 4:3).

In the previous verse, however, the Lord speaks of whoever serves him. Descriptions of effort, quality, and purity mentioned there may not be the only things to be considered. A number of qualifications are mentioned: "Therefore, O ye that embark in the service of God, see that ye serve him with all your heart, might, mind, and strength, that ye may stand blameless before God at the last day" (D&C 4:2).

To the thousands who can recite this verse from memory, the four offerings mentioned may be so familiar that the significance of them, as a picture of total dedication, may not be noticed. They are not just heart, might, mind, and strength, but they are (1) heart, (2) might, (3) mind, and (4) strength—a total of four. Together, they suggest complete, universal, and all-encompassing commitment. Thus, as we read this verse, we may ask, What will make one stand blameless before God at the last day? Answer: Total commitment and dedication to the work.

Other verses that can be considered while looking for this same message of inward commitment and duty include the following:

> Wherefore, I give unto them a commandment, saying thus: Thou shalt love the Lord thy God with all thy *heart*, with all thy *might*, *mind*, and *strength*; and in the name of Jesus Christ thou shalt serve him. (D&C 59:5; emphasis added)

> And thou shalt love the Lord thy God with all thy *heart*, and with all thy *soul*, and with all thy *mind*, and with all thy *strength*: this is the first commandment. (Luke 10:27; emphasis added)

> And he answering said, Thou shalt love the Lord
> thy God with all thy *heart*, and with all thy *soul*, and
> with all thy *strength*, and with all thy *might;* and thy
> neighbour as thyself. (2 Nephi 1:21; emphasis added)

> For verily the voice of the Lord is unto all men,
> and there is none to *escape*; and there is no *eye* that
> shall not see, neither *ear* that shall not hear, neither
> *heart* that shall not be penetrated. (D&C 1:2; empha-
> sis added)

> They are, however, to *warn, expound, exhort,* and
> *teach,* and invite all to come unto Christ. (D&C 20:59;
> emphasis added)

Does it not seem unusual, as well as beyond coincidence, that
the pattern God uses to outline the work of declaring the gospel
message is couched within the elements of four? Whether God
names the qualities of those who labor in His cause, or those
to whom the message is to be taken, or how it is to be taken,
He uses the number four. Casual reading may not identify significant messages other than the words themselves, but when the
symbolic message of the number four is added, a new dimension
comes into view.

Unto the Third and Fourth Generation

God has decreed numerous times that He will visit the iniquities of the fathers not only upon His people but also upon their
children. To the historian, it is evident that personal righteousness or unrighteousness, as well as the sins of parents, have an
effect upon the children. In studying the scriptures, we discover
how long this influence might be felt. Consider this sampling of
verses that include such proclamations:

> Thou shalt not bow down thyself to them, nor

serve them: for I the Lord thy God am a jealous God, visiting the iniquity of the fathers upon the children unto the *third* and *fourth* generation of them that hate me. (Exodus 20:5; emphasis added)

Keeping mercy for thousands, forgiving iniquity and transgression and sin, and that will by no means clear the guilty; visiting the iniquity of the fathers upon the children, and upon the children's children, unto the *third* and to the *fourth* generation. (Exodus 34:7; emphasis added)

The Lord is longsuffering, and of great mercy, forgiving iniquity and transgression, and by no means clearing the guilty, visiting the iniquity of the fathers upon the children unto the *third* and *fourth* generation. (Numbers 14:18; emphasis added)

If the justice of God is to be answered upon the children of the transgressor, will it only last to the fourth generation and not continue on to the fifth? What if you are in the fourth generation? Is there a chance that God's justice will extend only to those of the third generation?

Once again, applying the symbolic characteristics of numbers three and four, we can solve this doctrinal quandary. Consider the message of the number three discussed previously, contrasting the literal meaning with its symbolic meaning. The elements of fullness, completeness, and sufficiency are among those suggested by that number. Now apply these elements to the justice of God. Do they not match how we would expect God to deal with the effects of sin? Let the symbolic nature of the number speak.

Next, apply the elements suggested for the number four, which are universality and totality, with no boundaries of geography, race, or clime. Does this not describe how we would expect the judgments of God to apply? The question presents itself again: Is God trying to tell us, by using the numbers three and four, literally how many? Or is He communicating conditions, applications, and feelings about His judgments?

Examination of scriptures that use numbers two, three, four, or five, combined with the concept of *generations*, as in the previous examples, reveals an interesting picture. The following are the results of a survey of the number of verses that contain these terms:

	Bible	Book of Mormon	D&C	Total
Second Generation(s)	1	0	0	1
Third Generation(s)	2	0	0	2
Fourth Generation(s)	3	5	0	8
Third and Fourth Generation(s)	4	1	9	14
Fifth Generation(s)	0	0	0	0

Several of the numbers of verses used in conjunction with the idea of generations are certainly literal in nature, especially those in the Book of Mormon. However, even though they are literal, that does not preclude an additional symbolic message.

Another observation we might make concerns the number of times that *third* and *fourth* are used together. Why not just unto the fourth generation? Why does the Lord use both third and fourth simultaneously? We can conclude, as stated above, that these numbers are used to convey a message beyond the actual, or literal, number.

We can also conclude that the pattern of using numbers for the purpose of amplifying a message is no different than that of many present-day expressions. Many phrases we speak are not spoken to be numerically accurate as much as to communicate a message.

If a symbolic message is applied to verses that include "unto the third and fourth generation," a message comes forth that God will let the consequences of the sins of the fathers come upon the children fully, without partiality, and it will be universally applied in every condition and clime.

Such an interpretation precludes the harsh idea, which some people have, that God will bring nondiscriminating punishment to whomever falls within a given generation of descendants. Contrast that uncompromising message with the message that comes when applying the symbolism of numbers three and four—that God will reward any person fully and completely, in any generation, whenever and wherever that reward is deserved.

Conclusion

Use in the scriptures of the number four seems to point to the idea of including all God's children, Israelite and Gentile alike, of all ages and times. Besides having a physical application, the number four can be interpreted inwardly, for all the dimensions of the soul and the character. The number also suggests to the mind totality in commitment and effort. Nothing is to be exempt or held back. The idea includes all the elements of character as well geography and the dimensions of the universe.

5

The Number That Stands for Grace

Discovering the nature and uses of the number five is more challenging than discovering the same for the other single-digit numbers. The number five is not used as often as most others to communicate a symbolic message. This is the case for both the Bible and the additional scriptures of the restored Church. All these sacred records yield only a sprinkling of identifiable symbolic uses for the number five.

Due to this lack of use, Bible scholars who have written about the number five as a symbol do not agree on the interpretation of its symbolic message. Some say that its nature comes from combining the number two with the number three, giving the number a message combining the nature of those two numbers. Others say that the essence of the number five comes from combining the message of the number four with that of the number one.

Most agreement seems to be on the number five being used to convey a symbolic message of grace. The idea of grace emerges from having reached the universality and totality suggested by the number four and then moving beyond that to it only occurring by the grace of God. With so few instances of the number five being symbolically used by writers of scripture, we are left with a much dimmer picture of how we are to view its character. However, we can consider some examples.

The Grace of God

Examining the verses in which the number five is referenced provides reasons to associate it with the idea of grace. Those within the house or people of Israel are recipients of the grace of God as no other peoples. The story of Jacob, named Israel, in which he receives relief during a famine involves him and his sons.

First, Jacob's sons sold their brother Joseph into bondage to a caravan travelling to Egypt. However, Joseph rises by the grace of God to a position of favor and power in the Pharaoh's court. Eventually, Joseph's brothers come to Egypt seeking relief from the famine they are experiencing. While, most men would surely be tempted to exercise revenge, Joseph reveals himself to his brothers after he has them seated for a bounteous meal. They have come from famine-ravaged Canaan to Egypt, where Joseph has food stored in preparation for that very condition.

After Joseph's brothers are seated in the order of birth, Joseph gives some interesting directions about serving his brothers' food: "And he took and sent messes unto them from before him; but Benjamin's mess was five times so much as any of theirs. And they drank, and were merry with him" (Genesis 43:34).

Why did Joseph choose the number five or why did the recorder of the event use that number? The idea of grace seems to be a genuine possibility.

Afterward, Joseph gives each of his brothers changes of raiment, but to Benjamin he gives five changes (Genesis 45:22). When Joseph presents his brothers to the Pharaoh the first time, he presents five of them (Genesis 47:2). Undeserved favor seems to be one of the messages Joseph is trying to impress upon his brothers, and the word that best defines undeserved favor is grace.

The Hand and the Foot

With the idea of grace lingering in the mind, five can be related to the idea of a man working in accordance with God under His grace. A most common illustration of the number five occurs in the hand and foot of each person. Of course, each hand and foot contains five digits. The hand and foot of man are essential to so much of what we do that these body parts make excellent symbols.

The natural uses of the hand, with its four fingers, needs the thumb to become the expression of active power. Very little can be done by the fingers without the thumb. If you don't believe this, try it! Try to pick up something without using your thumb. Try to work or play without using your thumb. Try to create anything. Biblical people understood the significance of the thumb.

Conquered people often had the thumb of their right hand and the great toe of the right foot cut off by their victors (Judges 1:6). This seems to have been done for an assurance that they would not be able to effectively use weapons or run in aggressive action but would be confined to do menial labor that could be accomplished even with such impairments.

Conceivably, the four fingers represent all mankind and the thumb the one who empowers the other four. One who has the grace of God within thus makes the hand what it is, the tool for all work and effort.

If this message of grace is correct for the number five, it fits well when the sacrificial blood is placed upon the thumb of the right hand (Exodus 29:20). The blood would be from the offering that typified the offering of the great Jehovah. But the blood was not just put upon the thumb of the hand; it was also placed on the ear (one of the five senses) and on the big toe of the right foot. Thus comes the suggestion that this is man in his whole responsibility.

Supporting the idea of the number five being used symbolically to represent the concept of grace is the parable of the ten virgins (Matthew 25:1–13). Five virgins were foolish and five were wise. The five foolish virgins were not given grace and entrance into the wedding. On the other hand, the five wise virgins were welcomed and accommodated. To be invited and given entrance are both acts of grace by the marriage parties.

Abraham Found Grace

Seeking the grace of God is the greatest of challenges for any man. In the scriptures, we read that Abraham seeks such from God following his defeat of the kings who had captured his nephew Lot. Abraham pleads with God that he might have children or seed. God promises both seed and land to Abraham far beyond his greatest anticipations.

Abraham asks, "Whereby shall I know that I shall inherit it?" The Lord responds, "Take me an heifer of three years old, and a she goat of three years old, and a ram of three years old, and a turtledove, and a young pigeon" (Genesis 15:8, 9). Abraham was to offer these animals, five in number, to God. Is this number significant and symbolic?

Abraham knew that having posterity through his barren wife, Sarai, could only come by the grace of God, and now he was to receive lands that stretched from the Nile, the river of Egypt, to the great river called Euphrates.

The Pool of Bethesda

The pool of Bethesda was a place where the infirm waited in Jesus' day, hoping for an act of grace from God to heal them. This pool had five porches (John 5:2). Whether this was by architectural function or because of a symbolic message, we are left to wonder. However, the message of grace associated with the number five stands in the wings ready to take center stage if given the proper cue. Possibly this is why John included the name of the pool as well as the number of porches it had in his account (see Bible Dictionary, s.v. "Bethesda"). He was constantly trying to show that Jesus was the fulfillment of the Messianic dream and promise. Jesus' coming to the place of grace and telling a man to "Rise, take up thy bed, and walk" (John 5:8) takes new meaning and purpose when we know the message of the number five.

The House of Israel

The group of people upon which God had placed the greatest responsibility, as well as promised the greatest blessings, were the descendants of Jacob, whose name God changed to Israel. Therefore, the number five may well also represent the house of Israel, which uniquely held God's favor or grace. These comprised people who needed to be joined with God in His work as well as those who would listen to His word and walk in His paths.

The feeding of the five thousand (Matthew 14:15–21) may have been a feeding of a group of Israelites, and Matthew would understand this concept well. Contrast this number again with the feeding of the four thousand (Matthew 15:32–39). Should the reader of the text interpret these numbers as the actual number fed on each occasion?

To the literal reader, does it not seem more plausible for the account to read that the number fed was 4,957, or another, similar number? If such an exact count is not expected, then possibly the accounts should have recorded that the number of those fed was just over four thousand or nearly five thousand. After you feed so many with a small amount of food, the exact total may not be very significant. It would have been a miracle if only a hundred were fed with such small amounts of available provisions.

These same considerations can be applied to the amounts of the food gathered after everyone was filled. We could ask the question again at this point. Do the gospel writers use numbers to provide a literal record of the remaining food (twelve baskets), or do these numbers perhaps illustrate to whom Jesus gave spiritual nourishment (Matthew 14:20)? Possibly the story is much more than about miracles involving bread and fish. It may be even more meaningful for the gospel accounts to indicate whom it was that was fed and by what power they were fed. The number recorded is thus possibly more an indicator of who, rather than how many.

David's Work by the Grace of God

Is the number of stones that David chose out of the streambed with which he went to fight Goliath significant? He knew that if he were to defeat the giant, it would be by the grace of God. If he was so confident that God was going to help him, why didn't he pick up only one stone?

Read the account. "And he took his staff in his hand, and chose him five smooth stones out of the brook, and put them in a shepherd's bag which he had, even in a scrip; and his sling was in his hand: and he drew near to the Philistine" (1 Samuel 17:40).

David slew Goliath with his first stone, but he had five in his possession. The reader of the account gets a feeling for the power by which David had conquered the giant by paying attention to the number of stones chosen from the brook.

Conclusion

When our body reflects the scope of our daily living, when we use it because we have few other implements, when we depend on it totally, it becomes the object to which we relate everything else. Imagine the increased awareness of people who depend entirely on the fingers of the hand or toes of the foot. We would be significantly disadvantaged without them.

In addition, we can't work well without toes, let alone run or defend ourselves. We can't communicate and appreciate without the senses. Of course, in our society much has changed. Today, walking is supplanted by cars and cycles. If a person loses his feet, he can be transported by an electric cart. If a person loses one of his senses, an apparatus or aid is generally available for assistance.

As significant as our body parts and senses are to us today, we likely do not appreciate them and depend on them the way the people of the distant past did. Today we may be more hopeful about help from the government and our HMO than we are about the grace of God. But the grace of God was always present with His people—as present as their five senses, fingers, and toes.

6

The Number That Signifies Man and the World

The Bible begins its initial account with the number six taking center stage. The act being played out is the creation of heaven and earth and everything in them. These creative works of God took place in six days. Also of note in the creation drama is the specific day in which humankind, both male and female, is created—the sixth day. The message of the number six comes from this primary source of creation time, the message that six is the symbolic number for man and for man's labors.

Thus, not only does six appear predominantly in the creation, but six also constitutes the number of days within which man is to work and labor. On the other hand, one day out of seven is set aside for the Sabbath, a day that belongs to God. Therefore, the number six is associated with mortal man and the labors he is to perform by the sweat of his brow.

Additionally, there seems to be a correlation between man being required to labor for his sustenance during his mortal life and the law regarding servants. Under the law of Moses, every servant who had been bought was to be freed after six years of labor (Exodus 21:2; Deuteronomy 15:12; Jeremiah 34:14). We thus find a teachable concept behind every element of the Law of Moses. The idea of giving servants freedom after six years of servitude seems to match the idea of mortal man being bound to his labors for six days a week.

The Law of Moses includes other references to the number six besides man and servants. Under that, land was to be sown or used for six years. For the seventh year it was to lay fallow and unsown (Exodus 23:10, 11).

Man Is Mortal—Short of Perfection

When we consider the number seven in the next chapter, we will find it associated with perfection and completion. Because the number six is one less than the number seven, many who have written about numbers feel that the number six also denotes the idea of deficit or failure to reach the mark of perfection. Hence, the number six is symbolic of fallen mortal man. In his present condition, mortal man can never attain perfection.

One of the most referenced numbers in all of scripture involves the number six in the form of three sixes. That number appears in the Book of Revelation, in which John writes about seeing fierce-looking beasts. One beast will lead men into captivity and deceive many. It will also require a mark to be put upon people's right hand or forehead. John prophesied that in some future time, "No man might buy or sell, save he that had the mark, or the name of the beast, or the number of his name. Here is wisdom. Let him that hath understanding count the number of the beast: for it is the number of a man; and his number is Six hundred threescore and six" (Revelation 13:17–18).

The meaning of these numbers has been hotly debated. We could apply gemetria because of the phrase, "the number of his name." On the other hand, some want to identify the man as a specific person who might be alive. Others see the idea of six hundred three score and six being the symbol John uses to warn people who would live during the time of this beast. Beasts devour. Beasts cause havoc and terror. We should avoid such beasts at all costs.

What, then, might be the figurative parallel to the beast?

Something that should be feared because it devours. Symbolically associated with the number six is worldliness, the appetites of man in his mortal state. Worldliness, or "Babylon," is what God warns His children about the most. Why? Because it is the thing that is most devouring, that we should fear and avoid at all costs.

When considering whether the number six hundred three score and six should be read for its literal value or its symbolic message, we can be certain that the number six within it has a symbolic message. We can also note that the number is stamped upon all things human. However, the most compelling reason for a figurative interpretation are the surrounding expressions John uses whenever that number appears.

Why would a reader think that out of all the figurative beasts, wars, angels, horsemen, and such, this number—six hundred three score and six—was literal? Clearly, John and other biblical writers choose six as a number recognized universally as pertaining to man, in other words, a symbolic number.

In fact, three personages described in the Old Testament have the number six. These three characters portray things both evil and destructive. Moreover, the number six is used in each instance to describe something about them or what they did. The persons epitomize and portray images of evil.

- Nebuchadnezzar set up an image whose height was threescore cubits and the breadth was six cubits (Daniel 3:1).

- Pharaoh pursued the Israelites with six hundred chariots (Exodus 14:7).

- Goliath's height was listed as six cubits and a span (1 Samuel 17:4–7).

These individuals are types and shadows of things that are evil or things to be feared. These men from the past, as well as their names, are often used even today to depict things oppressive, overpowering, and evil.

The Deep Six

Words, phrases, and practices in our present culture exist that we seemingly know little about. One of these refers to burying the dead "six feet under." How literal is this practice? Investigation shows that burial seldom literally occurs that depth. Corpses are not typically buried six feet underground.

Likewise ships, when buried at sea, are given the "deep six." Think of the symbolism involved. The six periods of God's labor and the command that man should labor for six days are followed by a time wherein man—and God—should rest. The idea that man would have a period in which to perform all His labors, and then observe a sacred period to rest, seems to match with the symbolic idea of being placed to rest in a condition of six.

In summary, "The common symbolical meaning of this number seems to be incompleteness, imperfection, the falling short of the repose and bliss of the divine sabbatism" (*Bible Encyclopedia,* 100).

"The number six also connotes deficit, a failure to attain the completeness of seven, while eight designates superabundance. Symbolically forty-two is pejorative since, as one scholar has pointed out, it is the result of six multiplied by seven, i.e., perfection missing the mark'" (Draper, *Opening the Seven Seals,* 121).

Knowing that the number six symbolizes elements connected with mortal man, as well as man falling short of his desired goal, we are led joyously to the next single-digit number, which will take us to the mark or place of desired reward or excellence—the number seven.

7

The Number That Indicates Perfection

Moving naturally beyond things mortal and incomplete, we come to the number seven. The actual meaning of the word will be our first consideration.

In the Hebrew, seven is *shevah*. It is from the root *savah*, to be full or satisfied, to have enough. Hence, the meaning of the word *seven* is dominated by this root, for on the seventh day God rested from the work of creation. His work was full and complete, good and perfect. Nothing could be added to it or taken from it without marring it. Hence the word *shavath*, to cease, desist, rest, and *Shabbath, Sabbath,* or day of rest.

Seven—The Number Used Most Often As a Symbol

"The number seven is used so many times, outside normal mathematical numbers, that it can be easily noted for significance. The number seven has been the most easily identified number, as being figurative or symbolic. It has also been long established as the most prominent symbolic number" (*The International Standard Bible Encyclopedia*, 2159).

The number seven has found prominence not only in biblical writing but also in modern revelation and culture, both far and near. One publication on symbolism states:

> Use of the number seven extends far beyond just biblical expression. Its significance, sacred or otherwise, was widespread in the ancient East, especially in Babylonian culture. The number seven appears in several hundred scriptural passages and should be considered in a majority of those instances as symbolic. The number seven is representative of perfection and completeness. (Joseph Fielding McConkie and Donald W. Parry, *A Guide to Scriptural Symbols*, 99)

Should one then throw away the idea that the number seven never did mean six plus one? An answer to this question can possibly be found by reading the following statement, which indicates how biblical people felt about use of the number seven:

> When a man was said to have had 7 sons or daughters, or an action was reported as done or to be done 7 times, whether by design or accident, the number was noted, and its symbolic force remembered. It cannot indeed be regarded in all these cases as a sacred number, but its association with sacred matters which was kept alive among the Jews by the institution of the Sabbath, was seldom, if ever, entirely overlooked. (*The International Standard Bible Encyclopedia*, 2160)

Seven of This and Seven of That

Prominent uses of the number seven in scripture include the following: seven candles on the menorah lit the tabernacle and temple of ancient Israel (Exodus 25:31–32); seven priests compassed the city of Jericho seven times for seven days, blowing seven trumpets on the seventh (Joshua 6:4–15); Joseph interpreted a dream for the Egyptian pharaoh that indicated there would be seven good years of harvest followed by seven bad years (see Genesis 41:1–16); the same vision included seven ears of corn and seven kine, with the same message of seven years of plenty followed by seven years of famine (Genesis 41:14–54); there were seven altars and seven animals for the offering of sacrifices (Numbers 23:1,29; 28:11); the blood was sprinkled seven-fold on the Day of Atonement (Leviticus 16:14,19); the Lord's rejection and destruction of Saul and his house are complete with the demise of his seven sons (2 Samuel 21:6).

By applying the symbolism of the number seven, that of completeness and perfection, the following conclusions can be made: The light of the menorah in the tabernacle represents God and the way He lights our way so that we can see. As the menorah has seven candles, it suggests that God's light is perfect and complete. The seven priests circling the city of Jericho seven times for seven days shows complete obedience to what Joshua's people needed to do if they were to conquer Jericho and the land of Canaan. From the sevens in the Pharaoh's vision, Joseph could understand that the famine, as well as deliverance from the famine, would be complete. The seven sacrificial animals represent the Son of God, who was perfect and complete. The sacrifice, as well as the forgiveness for sins of those who made the offerings, was complete and perfect. And Saul, rejected while still on the throne, had sons who were destined for the throne, but his rejection was complete and final.

Jacob served seven years each for Rachel and Leah (Genesis 29:20, 27), and Jacob bowed seven times to his estranged brother Esau (Genesis 33:3). Samson had a seven-day marriage feast, had seven locks of hair, and was bound with seven withes (Judges 14:10–18, 16:7–8, 13). Naomi was told that Ruth's babe was "better to thee than seven sons" (Ruth 4:15).

We find seven horns and seven eyes mentioned in John's vision (Revelation 5:6). Seven heads in seven crowns are described later (Revelation 8:6; 12:3).

Into each of theses uses of the number seven, a message of perfection and completeness can be read, either for the event itself, for the people, or for the condition and circumstances that surround the incident.

The story about Jacob and his wives is of particular interest as we have just discussed the number six with its message of mortal man and his labors. The account tells that Jacob had gone to live with his mother's people in the land of Haran. He had fallen in love with Rachel, Laban's daughter, and asked for her hand in marriage. He offered to serve Laban seven years if he could marry Rachel. Laban promised to give her to him, and Jacob served the seven years for Rachel. However, on the night of their marriage, Laban put Rachel's older sister, Leah, who was veiled until they were together in the bedchamber, together with Jacob. Jacob thought that he was married to, as well as in the chamber with, Rachel, the love of his heart. But in the morning, he discovered that he was with Leah. Let us examine the dialogue that Jacob had with Laban.

> And Laban said, It must not be so done in our country, to give the younger before the firstborn.
>
> Fulfill her week, and we will give thee this also for the service which thou shalt serve with me yet seven other years.
>
> And Jacob did so, and fulfilled her week: and he gave him Rachel his daughter to wife also.
>
> And Laban gave to Rachel his daughter Bilhah his handmaid to be her maid.
>
> And he went in also unto Rachel, and he loved also Rachel more than Leah, and served with him yet seven other years. (Genesis 29:26–30)

We, of course, notice the sevens within these verses as well as within the "week" of seven days, and we wonder if they are literal or figurative numbers. Verse 20 states that "Jacob served seven years for Rachel; and they seemed unto him but a few days, for the love he had to her." But what if the numbers were figurative, having the message of perfection and completeness? Would the story be dealt a discrediting blow, or would it be enhanced with feelings of perfection and satisfaction?

While pondering that question, let us finish Jacob's story in Haran. Laban employs Jacob to be the husbandman of his numerous flocks. Jacob seems to be making Laban wealthy by his good management. But Jacob wants to return to the home of his birth. Laban then pleads for him to stay and offers Jacob a part of his flocks as payment. Jacob agrees, but sometime afterward he tells his wives that their father has changed his wages ten times. Thus, he is no longer bound and is going home.

Laban catches up with Jacob after he has journeyed some distance and wants to know why Jacob has suddenly departed. Jacob's answer is interesting in light of the symbolic messages of numbers six and seven. He says, "Thus have I been twenty years in thy house; I served thee fourteen years for thy two daughters, and six years for thy cattle" (Genesis 31:41).

The possibility that Jacob was telling exactly how long he served for both his wives and his cattle is noted. However, is it not also possible that he is using dualism, indicating what he served for and how he felt about the service? For each of his wives, his service was perfect and complete because of what he received as payment. His service for the flocks, which were things of man, was six years. Now, it was time to be freed from his servitude, and his reward had been the things of the world. It was time for Jacob to rest and have a sabbath away from his labors under Laban. What a powerful message these symbolic numbers add!

Seven and Six Used Together

One of the proverbs uses the number seven in an interesting way, by listing the evils of man:

> These six things doth the Lord hate: yea, seven are an abomination unto him:
> A proud look, a lying tongue, and hands that shed innocent blood,
> An heart that deviseth wicked imaginations, feet that be swift in running to mischief,
> A false witness that speaketh lies, and he that soweth discord among brethren. (Proverbs 6:16–19)

The author of the proverb says there are six things but then lists seven. Surely there is a reason for making such an obvious misstatement or report. Why does the writer use both the number six and the number seven as he lists seven things?

Note again what he says: "These *six* things doth the Lord hate: yea, *seven* are an abomination unto him: [1] A proud look, [2] a lying tongue, and [3] hands that shed innocent blood, [4] An heart that deviseth wicked imaginations, [5] feet that be swift in running to mischief, [6] A false witness that speaketh lies, and [7] he that soweth discord among brethren" (Proverbs 6:16–19; emphasis added).

A possible answer is that because seven actions are listed, we have an indication that the list is complete, that if one avoids those seven things, sin will be avoided, without exception. The use of the number six, most likely, is used to emphasize that these are not things of the spirit but actions of the mortal. Combining these two numbers in this manner may well be an effort to contrast that which is human with what is spiritual. The message of the number six is incompleteness and imperfection of man or mortal things. The number seven moves an individual's mind and heart to the idea of reaching a goal, of finishing and reaching perfection.

The reader of the proverb can see that the list includes the beginning passions that initiate every offense toward God and others. With the symbolic nature of both numbers understood somewhat, it is logical and proper to have them both included with the list of sins the Lord hates. Each number suggests a message, a message that is more important than knowing how many sins are on God's list of the downfalls of man.

Job likely had this same message in mind when he composed the words found in his book. He wrote, "He shall deliver thee in six troubles: yea, in seven there shall no evil touch thee" (Job 5:19).

The same combination of these two numbers seems also to be operational in Hosea's account of Israel's lovers. Israel's false lovers give only six things while Jehovah gives seven (Hosea 2:5–9).

Seven in Feasts and Celebration

The seventh day of the week was different from the other days of the week. It was holy. The Feast of Tabernacles comprised seven days (Leviticus 23:34), and the Feast of Passover and the eating of unleavened bread also comprised seven days (Exodus 34:18). The seventh year was the sabbatical year (Exodus 23:10–11).

Relative to the creation of the earth and the seventh day, the Sabbath day or day of rest, one verse in Genesis is fascinating. It states, "On the seventh day God ended his work which he had made; and he rested on the seventh day from all his work which he had made" (Genesis 2:2).

The fascinating question seems to be: Why does it not say that God finished His work on the sixth day rather than on the seventh? The sixth day was the day that "God saw every thing that he had made" (Genesis 1:31). In the above instance, it may well be that the account seeks to communicate to the reader that everything God made was perfect and complete.

Sometimes people wonder whether it is good to have certain things that are harmful to us here on the earth but usable to mankind. However, the symbolism of the number seven is helpful in teaching us that God created things perfectly and completely. He made no mistakes in what he put here for us, ending His work on the seventh day.

Seven in Cleansing and Purification

When dealing with real or suspected uncleanness through leprosy, the presence of a corpse, or with other incidents of possible contagion, seven days of seclusion was necessary. Naaman was told to bathe seven times in the River Jordan (2 Kings 5:10). Peter asked if one should forgive seven times. He was told to forgive seventy times seven, an amplification of seven (Matthew 18:21, 22). The symbolism of the number seven applied to these events surely adds meaning. Cleansing and purifying do not occur when the person does so less than completely.

Stories Using Seven

After Elijah defeated the priests of Baal on Mount Carmel, he took his servant apart and prayed that God would break the drought and bless the earth with rain. He promised King Ahab that rain was forthcoming. The account states, "[He] said to his servant, Go up now, look toward the sea. And he went up, and looked, and said, There is nothing. And he said, Go again seven times" (1 Kings 18:43).

We most likely must choose between two ideas: either we are to believe that the servant counted the number of times he went to look, or we can believe that the servant perfectly obeyed the instructions of Elijah and did so until a perfect result was observed. The manner of describing the action of his looking, or the desired end of what he did, was that he looked seven times. That was also the message of the Savior and the law—to forgive seven times, and then seventy times seven.

Today, we might say, "I've told you a dozen times." The message is not that we have literally counted the number of times instructions were given as much as it is that the person we're talking to should understand.

Notice the next verse in Elijah's account: "And it came to pass at the seventh time, that he said, Behold, there ariseth a little cloud out of the sea, like a man's hand. And he said, Go up, say unto Ahab, Prepare thy chariot, and get thee down, that the rain stop thee not" (1 Kings 18:44).

In the next chapter of the story, Elijah is told to anoint a new king and a new prophet. However, Elijah tells God that the children of Israel have forsaken the covenant, thrown down God's altars, and slain God's prophets, so that he alone is left. Now, however, God wants Elijah to know something. He says, "Yet I have left me seven thousand in Israel, all the knees which have not bowed unto Baal, and every mouth which hath not kissed him" (1 Kings 19:18).

Both of these idioms, "knees which have not bowed" and "mouth which hath not kissed" are figurative, so why should the number seven thousand be considered differently? Could there have been a count of the knees that had not bowed or the mouths that had not kissed? If there was an accounting made, even by God, does it not seem too coincidental that it would be exactly seven thousand?

The symbolic viewpoint would ask whether there were more than one message that Elijah and the people should know from this statement? The answer: Because of the use of the word *thousand*, we should know that Elijah is far from being the only remaining faithful one. Because of the use of the number *seven*, Elijah should know that this large group of people who have not turned away from Jehovah are completely or fully obedient, and there is thus no reason for Elijah not to move ahead in his service.

If we were to know that there were precisely seven thousand faithful, in addition to the other items of information, then wonderful. But the number seven that has been considered goes far beyond the literal telling of exactly how many.

The same consideration could be applied to the accounts of a woman marrying seven times, with each husband dying, and the Sadducees wanting the Savior to indicate which husband she would end up with in the next life (Mark 12:18–27; Luke 20:27–38). Neither the question nor the answer would have changed if she had married more or less times than seven. But that is the point. By using the symbolic number of completeness, the hearer of the story knows that the point in question did not have anything to do with the actual number of men or marriages. The question dealt with other principles and doctrines.

The same question of literal vs. figurative emerges from the story of Shadrach, Meshach, and Abednego. Nebuchadnezzar puts the three men into a fiery furnace. Because he had placed them in positions of trust and power and they did not conform to the edicts given to his people, Nebuchadnezzar commanded that the furnace be heated beyond the normal temperature. He gave the order "that they should heat the furnace seven times more than it was wont to be heated" (Daniel 3:19).

If that direction and temperature were to be taken literally, some things would have been needful. First, the people of the time must have had a way to measure the heat. This was generally done by watching the color of the fire. However, the ability to measure the temperature and then raise that temperature seven times is highly questionable. Second, if the kindling temperature of wood, generally between seven hundred and eight hundred degrees, was increased to seven times that amount, that would result in a temperature approaching six thousand degrees. That would melt the rock of the furnace and the sand of the pit.

A literal understanding of the number seven in this story seems impossible. However, a symbolic meaning leads to a powerful message regarding the virtues of the story. The furnace was heated completely, perfectly, absolutely. There was nothing about the fire that could allow the escape of the three young Hebrews except the power of God. So we shouldn't look at the fire as the central element of the story but rather look to God.

Isaiah prophesied that the Kingdom of Judah would become so apostate that it would be difficult to find a faithful man to whom a woman could look for protection, sustenance, and moral leadership. The picture Isaiah painted is so disparaging that he writes, "And in that day seven women shall take hold of one man, saying, We will eat our own bread, and wear our own apparel: only let us be called by thy name, to take away our reproach" (Isaiah 4:1).

So many have wanted to interpret this verse literally. Their conclusion is that some day a man should expect that he would have seven women married to him. This conclusion, while possible, must give way to the possibility that Isaiah might have been telling his people that the day would come when it would be very difficult to find a faithful husband. The apostasy would be so complete that priesthood leadership and security would be virtually gone. The desire of women of the covenant would be so great to have a faithful husband that they would do anything in order not to marry someone unworthy and thus incur God's reproach.

John the Beloved's Use of the Number Seven

In the book of Revelation, written by John, we read of seven stars, seven angels, seven candlesticks, seven seals, seven horns, seven eyes, seven heads, and seven crowns. John speaks to the seven churches, even though we know from historical sources that there were other branches of the church besides the seven that are mentioned.

In the gospel of John, careful readers find and identify structure and organization that John has carefully integrated within his record. Themes have been identified. The first being the duel between light (Christ and His ways) and darkness (Satan and the ways of the world). The second theme deals with the issues of water and life. In his gospel, John shows Christ as having power over water. The significance of water to any locale was important, but to Palestine it was essential. If Jesus had power over water, He must be God in the flesh. John includes seven examples of Jesus' power dealing with water. Note the following:

1. Jesus turns water into wine (John 2:1–11).

2. Jesus gives a discourse on living waters at Jacob's well (John 4:5–14).

3. Jesus heals an invalid man at the pool of Bethesda (John 5:2–9).

4. Jesus walks on the water at Galilee (John 6:16–21).

5. Jesus offers living water during the Feast of Tabernacles (John 7:37–39).

6. Jesus heals the man born blind at the Pool of Siloam (John 9:1–7).

7. Jesus washes the feet of the twelve (John 13:4, 5).

The possibility of John selecting these seven incidents to make a point is furthered by details within the third theme noted in his gospel, involving seven signs and seven discourses. John records:

1. Changing the water into wine (John 2:1–11).
2. Restoring life to the nobleman's son (John 4:4–54).
3. Healing the invalid on the Sabbath (John 5:2–9).
4. Feeding the multitude (John 6:2–13).
5. Walking on the water (John 6:16–21).
6. Healing the man born blind (John 9:1–7).
7. Raising Lazarus from the dead (John 11:1–45).

1. The natural man is converted into a spiritual man (John 3:3–8).
2. Living waters bring everlasting life (John 4:5–14).
3. Jesus is Lord of the Sabbath (John 5: 9–16).
4. "I am the bread of life" (John 6:26–51).
5. Christ, who will walk into the presence of the Father, offers living water to all (John 7:37–39).
6. Christ is the light of the world (John 8:12).
7. "I am the good shepherd: the good shepherd giveth his life for the sheep" (John 10:11).

The possibility that John included in his testimony a designed number of incidents seems plausible. The message of the number seven, added to the message of the incidents themselves, adds intensity, purpose, and meaning to John's words. John conveyed the message that it was perfectly clear and perfectly proven that Jesus was the promised Messiah.

Half of Perfection and Completion

With this understanding of the number seven, we can observe the prophetic use of the designation *three and one-half*. Richard Draper writes that three and a half should be thought of as half of seven, the number that symbolizes perfection. Such halving of the number seven represents a fullness of imperfection (Draper, *Opening the Seven Seals,* 138).

The idea of one-half of something is often used in present-day idioms such as, "He's a half wit," or "He is just a half pint of a guy." When someone performs with less than full effort, he might be described as "half-hearted." These expressions generally describe quality more than actual quantity. They use the idea of half as a symbol of things lacking or imperfect.

We see this in Revelation 11:9, 11. The three-and-a-half-year drought pronounced upon Israel by Elijah should also be noted, as recorded in 1 Kings 17:1; 18:1. Passages that employ half of the number seven, with the corresponding number of months (forty-two), should be read with this idea of incompleteness in mind. Many readers attempt to identify these symbolic numbers as literal. However, a wiser interpretation would be to look at them as symbols.

Symbols are meant to represent an unspoken message rather than to be understood literally. Symbolism should be applied not only to the number seven but also to the halving of that number. The number forty-two is also the result of fourteen multiplied by three, as used by Matthew in his gospel account of the lineage of Jesus. Although here the number forty-two results from a much different source than taking half of seven years, both instances should, nonetheless, be examined for their figurative messages. Perhaps the number forty-two in Jesus' lineage represents only half of the equation, namely His imperfect earthly lineage, not His heavenly one through His Father in Heaven.

The Abrahamic Covenant

When God called Abram out of the land of his father to a new life, God made certain promises to him. One of these was that he, Abram, would receive a new name, Abraham. His wife's name would also be changed from Sarai to Sarah.

In addition, God blessed this patriarch with seven blessings (Genesis 12:2–3; 17). The Book of Abraham was recorded on a parchment and, in the nineteenth century, given to the Prophet Joseph Smith, who translated it. Comparisons made between the translation made by Joseph Smith and the biblical account show significant differences.

The book of Abraham records:

> And I will make of thee a great nation, and I will bless thee above measure, and make thy name great among all nations, and thou shalt be a blessing unto thy seed after thee, that in their hands they shall bear this ministry and Priesthood unto all nations;
>
> And I will bless them through thy name; for as many as receive this Gospel shall be called after thy name, and shall be accounted thy seed, and shall rise up and bless thee, as their father;
>
> And I will bless them that bless thee, and curse them that curse thee; and in thee that is, in thy Priesthood and in thy seed that is, thy Priesthood, for I give unto thee a promise that this right shall continue in thee, and in thy seed after thee that is to say, the literal seed, or the seed of the body shall all the families of the earth be blessed, even with the blessings of the Gospel, which are the blessings of salvation, even of life eternal. (Abraham 2:9–11)

Even though differences exist between the Genesis and the Book of Abraham narratives, the same seven promises stand out in both accounts:

1. I will make of thee a great nation.

2. I will bless thee above measure.

3. I will make thy name great among all nations.

4. Thou shalt be a blessing unto thy seed after thee that in their hands they shall bear this ministry and Priesthood unto all nations.

5. I will bless them through thy name; for as many as receive this Gospel shall be called after thy name, and shall be accounted thy seed.

6. I will bless them that bless thee and curse them that curse thee.

7. In thee that is, in thy Priesthood and in thy seed that is thy Priesthood, for I give unto thee a promise that this right shall continue in thee, and in thy seed after thee that is to say, the literal seed, or the seed of the body shall all the families of the earth be blessed.

This sevenfold blessing, in and of itself, is overwhelming. What must Abraham have felt? However, possibly additional meaning and understanding came to him by realizing the seven elements of the promise, suggesting perfectness and completeness. Certainly, the same message can come to one today who bears the name of Abraham. Those promises can be assessed and applied with the feelings of that same message of completeness and perfection!

8

The Number That Emulates Mercy

When progressing through the numbers and trying to catch the uniqueness of each one, we move past the number seven, which suggested perfection and completeness. Now anything beyond this idea is a bonus! It would be obtained only by mercy and benevolence. It also would be beyond the finish mark and, thus, like a new beginning. After reaching the pinnacle of seven, it would be like starting over again. Therefore, it is a bit like seven plus one or, of course, the number eight. That is the nature of this number. Its message is of a new beginning or new life, which comes only by the mercy and benevolence of God

Under the Law of Moses, use of the number seven includes lepers who, after they are pronounced clean on the seventh day, are permitted to bring the offerings of purification on the eighth day. At that time, they are completely reinstated to a full association with others.

Similar to this phenomenon is the eighth day after the Feast of Tabernacles, which lasted a week (Numbers 29:35; Leviticus 23:36). This eighth day was the day on which the firstlings of the harvest were presented to God. It thus represented the conclusion of a cycle of festivals and the opening of new ones. On the eighth day, a new order of things commenced.

From the eighth day of the presentation of the first fruits, for example, seven weeks were to be counted. This feast of weeks, or second harvest, was to be kept, not on the seven times seventh day but on the fiftieth day. The notation of a fiftieth day is another form of referencing an eighth day. The eighth day was significant. On this day the firstborn of clean animals was made holy unto God (Exodus 22:30). Also on the eighth day, Aaron and his sons were to offer God their sacrifice that by fire (Leviticus 9:1, 2).

Circumcision and Baptism

Circumcision was another practice connected with the number eight. This ritual, symbolizing the beginning of a new life and becoming a part of Israel, was performed on the eighth day of life for a newborn male Israelite child. Circumcision was a precursor, an outward reminder, performed at eight days of age, that a newness of life associated with baptism was to follow at the age of eight years.

Joseph Smith added information to the text of the King James Bible that dealt with circumcision. The changes appear in Genesis 17. Careful reading notes that his edited text declares that baptism is a requirement and that children are to be baptized at age eight. Joseph's text also gives the reason for circumcision being performed at the age of eight days. The Joseph Smith account is as follows:

> When Abram was ninety years old and nine, the Lord appeared to Abram, and said unto him, I am the Almighty God, give unto thee a commandment; that thou shalt walk uprightly before me, and be perfect.
>
> And I will make my covenant between me and thee, and I will multiply thee exceedingly.
>
> And it came to pass, that Abram fell on his face, and called upon the name of the Lord.
>
> And God talked with him, saying, My people have gone astray from my precepts, and have not kept mine ordinances, which I gave unto their fathers;
>
> And they have not observed mine anointing, and the burial, or baptism wherewith I commanded them;
>
> But have turned from the commandment, and

taken unto themselves the washing of children, and the blood of sprinkling;

And have said that the blood of the righteous Abel was shed for sins; and have not known wherein they are accountable before me.

As for me, behold, my covenant is with thee, and thou shalt be a father of many nations.

And this covenant I make, that thy children may be known among all nations. Neither shall thy name any more be called Abram, but thy name shall be called Abraham; for, a father of many nations have I made thee.

And I will make thee exceedingly fruitful, and I will make nations of out thee, and kings shall come of thee.

And I will establish a covenant of circumcision with thee, and it shall be my covenant between me and thee, and thy seed after thee, in their generations; that thou mayest know for ever that children are not accountable before me until they are eight years old.

And thou shalt observe to keep all my covenants wherein I covenanted with thy fathers; and thou shalt keep the commandments which I have given thee with mine own mouth, and I will be a God unto thee and thy seed after thee.

And I will give unto thee and thy seed after thee, a land wherein thou art a stranger; all the land of Canaan, for an everlasting possession; and I will be their God.

And God said unto Abraham, Thou shalt keep my covenant, Therefore thou, and thy seed after thee in their generations.

This is my covenant which ye shall keep, between me and you and thy seed after thee; Every man-child among you shall be circumcised.

And ye shall circumcise the flesh of your foreskin; and it shall be a token of the covenant betwixt me and you.

And he that is eight days old shall be circumcised among you, every man child in your generations, he that is born in thy house, or bought with money of any stranger, which is not of thy seed.

He that is born in thy house, and he that is bought with thy money, must needs be circumcised, and my covenant shall be in your flesh for an everlasting covenant.

And the uncircumcised man child, whose flesh of his foreskin is not circumcised, that soul shall be cut off from his people; he hath broken my covenant. (JST, Genesis 17:1–18)

Symbolism involved with baptism points to the idea that the individual being baptized is being reborn (John 3:5–7). Hence, the age set by the Lord is not seven years of age, or six, or nine, but the age of a new beginning or new life. This new beginning comes only by the mercy of a most benevolent God. The new beginning of baptism sets one on the path of a clean, new life, free from sin, because those younger than eight years old are said, by the Lord, to be innocent and are covered by the mercy of God (Moroni 8:8–22; D&C 68:25; D&C 137:10).

With baptism, those who are age eight can now continue in their innocence. Because of this ordinance they are likewise covered by the mercy of God. Parents are directed that it is their responsibility to see that their children are taught and given the opportunity to be baptized at eight years of age (D&C 68:25).

The Transfiguration and Resurrection

The New Testament records that the Transfiguration took place on the eighth day following the Savior's feeding and teaching the thousands (Luke 9:28). This event seemed the beginning, for those present, of a new age with "the power and coming of our Lord Jesus Christ" (2 Peter 1:16).

Similarly, an event that solidified God's work following the redeeming work of atonement and resurrection took place on an eighth day. It was on the day that Jesus appeared to all of His disciples together. Jesus now began His own new life; His body was resurrected. John records this event as follows: "And after eight days again his disciples were within, and Thomas with them: then came Jesus, the doors being shut, and stood in the midst, and said, Peace be unto you" (John 20:26). It was at this event that the Savior gave His apostles courage and direction that carried them back to Galilee and throughout their ministries.

The same kind of message is contained in the Savior's rising on the first day of the week. The first day of the week should be looked at as the eighth day as it follows the seventh day, Saturday.

This new beginning must be remembered with its enormous consequences. Christ's rising was the first of any rising. His rising from the tomb meant that each of us will also experience a new beginning. In addition, we must remember that it is by the mercy of God that we will all rise from the grave, that it is granted to each of us because He broke the bands of death. This was done on the eighth day of the week.

Appearing before the Mercy Seat

We should think of the number eight as a symbol of new life, a new era, a new beginning. As mentioned, however, we should also consider what is behind all such events. What gives new life? What gives new eras and beginnings? God's mercy! In His graciousness and kindness, His tenderness and His love, He provides new beginnings and life. Therefore, the message of the number eight is mercy. New beginnings come and are given because of mercy.

With this thought in mind, consider the following: The place of mercy best known in ancient Israel was the mercy seat. This mercy seat was the top lid of the ark of the covenant, upon which were positioned two cherubs or angels. One was positioned on each end of the lid or mercy seat of the ark. The wings of each angel arched toward the center and touched the wings of the opposite cherub. The ark of the covenant was positioned near an altar of sacrifice in the temple in Jerusalem on a porch or pedestal. This porch had eight altars or tables upon which sacrifices were prepared.

The porch, appropriately, had eight steps upon which the priest had to ascend as he approached the mercy seat and participated in offerings resulting in God's mercy. Ezekiel described the gloriousness of the temple structure this way. He wrote:

> And the arches thereof were toward the outward court; and palm trees were upon the posts thereof, on this side, and on that side: and the going up to it had eight steps. . . .
> And the posts thereof were toward the utter court; and palm trees were upon the posts thereof, on this side, and on that side: and the going up to it had eight steps. . . .
> Four tables were on this side, and four tables on that side, by the side of the gate; eight tables, whereupon they slew their sacrifices. (Ezekiel 40:34, 37, 41)

Eight steps led up to the mercy seat. Imagine the message that would come to the mind and heart as an individual approached the place of sacrifice. The sacrifice was generally for personal expiation of sins or for those of all Israel. When offering such sacrifice, people knew that such forgiveness was based upon the mercy of a most gracious God.

The Brother of Jared, Ships, and Stones

The brother of Jared had to prepare sixteen small stones to provide light for the barges in which he and his companions were to travel. Theirs was to be a perilous journey and would be accomplished only by the actions of a merciful God.

How many vessels were there? "And it came to pass that the brother of Jared (now the number of the vessels which had been prepared was eight), went forth unto the mount, which they called the mount Shelem, because of its exceeding height, and did molten out of a rock sixteen small stones; and they were white and clear, even as transparent glass; and he did carry them in his hands upon the top of the mount, and cried again unto the Lord" (Ether 3:1).

Maybe they literally needed eight vessels. But should we also look for a symbolic message in that number? There doesn't seem to be a conclusive answer. However, eight is mentioned, and a possibility exists that there was a message that could be present with this number relative to the mercy of God, and that these people were beginning life anew on a land God, in His mercy, had prepared for them.

This same logic can be applied to the record of Nephi, in which he recounts the many hardships his family encounters in living and traveling through the wilderness from their home in Jerusalem. They are about to embark into a new beginning. They are going to leave the land of Palestine and go by ship to a new land. As the record shows, this new land will be obtained only by the mercy of God. Nephi records, "And we did sojourn for the space of many years, yea, even eight years in the wilderness" (1 Nephi 17:4).

Nephi's manner of writing, first mentioning that they had traveled many years and then giving the specific number eight, seems unusual. This is particularly so when we know that Nephi is concerned enough with having sufficient room on his plates that he uses language carefully and avoids excesses so that he doesn't multiply words (Mormon 9:32–33; 1 Nephi 19:6).

However, this verse seems to be an example of excess wording. If he wanted to tell precisely how many years they had journeyed, why did he not just say that they sojourned for eight years? If he wanted to tell that they had sojourned for an undetermined number of years, why did he also include the specific number eight? Is it possible that he wanted to indicate, by using a symbolic number, that their many years of sojourn were accomplished only by the tender mercies of God and that the new beginning upon which they were now embarking would be achieved only because of that same source of divine help? The possibility of such a message seems likely.

We might apply this same reasoning to the account of Ammon, in which he tells of helping the people of Limhi escape from bondage to the wicked Lamanites. Knowing that their miraculous escape is painted with the brush of God's mercy, it seems fitting for the account to read as follows:

"And the Lord did strengthen them, that the people of King Noah could not overtake them to destroy them. And they fled eight days journey into the wilderness" (Mosiah 23:2–3).

When considering the use of numbers, the question is whether or not the message dictated by the use of the number is literal or figurative. Would it make any difference in Ammon's story if the account mentioned that they journeyed six, ten, or ninety days journey if a literal interpretation were chosen? They didn't arrive at any place of significance. They didn't return to this place after they left it. Never is there a mention in the account of anyone wondering where this place was, nor is there mention of how this people knew that they had journeyed eight days.

However, if the message of the account is figurative and communicates mercy and a new beginning, such a message would not appear if a number other than the number eight were used. The possibility of both a literal and symbolic use of numbers in these accounts is also likely. However, to look at numbers only in a literal manner may leave the reader without the deeper meaning possibly intended by the authors.

Bread upon the Waters

Without some understanding of the use of numbers, we are at a loss when trying to find meaning to several scriptural verses. However, when we know the symbolic use of a number, images

may possibly come to our minds and hearts that could not other-
wise come. For example, the preacher in Ecclesiastes wrote, "Cast
your bread upon the waters; for thou shalt find it after many days.
Give a portion to seven, also to eight; for thou knowest not what
evil shall be upon the earth" (Ecclesiastes 11:1–2).

Could this verse be suggesting that if we are going to cast
our bread (charity) upon the waters, we should do it completely
(seven)? We should do this if we expect bread to mercifully (eight)
return to us.

Conclusion

In summarizing the number eight and its message, we have
noted that we are baptized for the remission of our sins, which
comes to us only through the mercy of God. We will rise from the
grave because of the mercy of God, just as Jesus rose on the eighth
day of the week. The message of the number eight is mercy. It follows perfection and completion (number seven) and thus denotes
a new beginning.

9

The Number That Reflects Judgment

Characteristics unique to the number nine help us as we seek for the symbolic use of this number. The number of times this number is used in scriptures does not provide abundant sampling. However, some things known about the number itself may give direction as to its use and figurative connotation. Not only does the number nine have distinctive character traits, but it also has mathematical elements that make it stand by itself. If these unique characteristics can be identified, then we have our best chance of discovering or determining what, if any, are the symbolic uses for this number.

As we appraise the single-digit numbers, we determine that nine is the second of the single-digit numbers that are the product of squaring its primary factor. Four is the first such number, and the number four is the result of squaring its primary factor, which is two ($2 \times 2 = 4$). Nine is the second such number and results from the squaring of three ($3 \times 3 = 9$). However, even though they are alike in this peculiarity, their likeness ends there because not only is four 2×2, but it is also is $2 + 2$. The number nine, on the other hand, is 3×3, while $3 + 3 = 6$.

Thus, even though they are alike in one aspect, they are not alike in all classifications. Because the number nine is the square of a primary number but not the sum of the two factors, this number is like no other. However, the distinction between number nine and other numbers can be taken a step further. Both results, the nine by multiplying the factors and the six by adding the factors, can be multiplied. The result is fifty-four (6 X 9 = 54). And the digits of the resulting answer added together also equal nine.

Applying the system of gemetria, as discussed briefly in the introduction, to the result of multiplying the numbers six and nine is intriguing. This process of giving weight to each letter of the alphabet assigns the number nine to the name Dan. In addition to its gematrial number, the name Dan has a meaning and is a metonymical name, just like other prominent names in the Bible.

And what is the meaning for the word or name Dan? Remember what Rachel, the wife of Jacob, said at the birth of Jacob's fifth son? Each of those sons, as well as all those who followed, was given a name that represented something pertinent to the life of the family. "And Rachel said, God hath judged me, and hath also heard my voice, and hath given me a son; therefore called she his name Dan" (Genesis 30:6).

Notice that she said that God had "judged me." The literal meaning of the name Dan is *He has judged*. As we read further, we discover that when Jacob was nearing death, he gave each of his sons a blessing. In the blessing to Dan, he said, "Dan shall judge his people, as one of the tribes of Israel" (Genesis 49:16).

When a symbol is established for someone or something, a relationship exists between the symbol and the object of the symbol. By studying the scriptures, we can certainly find evidence that a relationship exists between *Dan* and *judge*. We can also determine that the weight for the name Dan is nine. So, can the number nine help with judging?

Nine Can Always Help Us Judge

We can do something with the number nine that cannot be done with any other number, a helpful hint that math teachers love to pass on to their students. Multiply nine by any other number you choose; let's use 8 as an example. The equation would be 9 X 8 = 72. If you want to make sure you've arrived at the correct answer, simply add the numbers in the answer together, and if they total nine, you are correct!

When you try it with other numbers, you'll discover the following:

9 X 2 = 18. Check by adding 1 + 8 = 9 The digits add up to nine, so the answer is correct.

9 X 4 = 36. Check by adding 3 + 6 = 9.

9 X 15 = 135. Check by adding 1 + 3 + 5 = 9.

9 X 27 = 243. Check by adding 2 + 4 + 3 = 9.

9 X 456 = 4,104. Check by adding 4 + 1 + 0 + 4 = 9.

What a phenomenon! And it works every time, an easy way to double-check your answer every time. Will it work with only the small numbers? Let's see:

9 X 5,456 = 49,104. Does it work? Because this answer is large, we must reduce it to a single digit number. First add 4 + 9 + 1 + 0 + 4 = 18. Now add the 1 + 8 = 9. It works!

9 X 8,879,758 = 79,917,822. Once again, because the answer is large we must reduce it to a two-digit number. Add the 7 + 9 + 9 + 1 + 7 + 8 + 2 + 2 = 45. Add 4 + 5, and the sum is 9!

Nine and Ninety-Nine

Now, let's apply this concept to situations where the number nine is used in the scriptures. One such instance is in Luke 17. Luke not only places the number nine as a featured character on his stage, but he also uses this number to provoke the deepest questions. Most other numbers remain backstage while the number nine gets to be part of the drama along with the numbers one and ten. Is there a significance to the number nine playing its assigned role? Luke writes:

> And it came to pass, as he went to Jerusalem, that he passed through the midst of Samaria and Galilee.
> And as he entered into a certain village, there met him ten men that were lepers, which stood afar off:

> And they lifted up their voices, and said, Jesus, Master, have mercy on us.
>
> And when he saw them, he said unto them, Go shew yourselves unto the priests. And it came to pass, that, as they went, they were cleansed.
>
> And one of them, when he saw that he was healed, turned back, and with a loud voice glorified God,
>
> And fell down on his face at his feet, giving him thanks: and he was a Samaritan.
>
> And Jesus answering said, Were there not ten cleansed? But where are the nine?
>
> There are not found that returned to give glory to God, save this stranger.
>
> And he said unto him, Arise, go thy way: thy faith hath made thee whole. (Luke 17:11–19)

One question that seems appropriate regarding this event is, Why was this story told and recorded? Was Luke trying to get the listener to make a judgment? If so, what judgment? The most alarming element of the story seems to be that those who should have been more thankful were not. In fact, it was the Samaritan, one who was not expecting a Messiah such as Jesus, who returned to give thanks. Every reader most likely asks, Which one am I most like? Now, that's a powerful judgment!

The story of the lost sheep is another instance. Could this parable be inviting judgment from those who read it? If so, what question would initiate such judging? The story of the lost sheep goes as follows:

> And he spake this parable unto them, saying,
>
> What man of you, having an hundred sheep, if he lose one of them, doth not leave the ninety and nine in the wilderness, and go after that which is lost, until he find it?
>
> And when he hath found it, he layeth it on his shoulders, rejoicing.
>
> And when he cometh home, he calleth together his friends and neighbours, saying unto them, Rejoice

with me; for I have found my sheep which was lost.

I say unto you, that likewise joy shall be in heaven over one sinner that repenteth, more than over ninety and nine just persons, which need no repentance. (Luke 15:3–7)

Every soul who reads or hears this memorable parable must make the judgment: Am I a lost sheep? And every soul must ask, Will the Good Shepherd come looking for me, and when He finds me, will He rejoice over me? These questions concerning judgment seem to be linked to the number nine. Furthermore, the answers to these questions are as provable as are the answers to numbers being multiplied by the number nine.

Some, for example, may question the difference between the numbers nine and ninety-nine. While literally they are not the same, in gematria, they are identical. In gematria, you reduce multiple digits to a single digit. You do that by adding all the digits together. That would be $9 + 9 = 18$, and again you would add $1 + 8 = 9$. The two numbers may thus be much more alike than they would seem.

Remember also that Abraham was ninety-nine years old and Sarah was ninety years old when they were told the extraordinary news, that in their old age they would bear a son upon whom God would place His covenant—not Ishmael but a son whom they named Isaac (Genesis 17:15–21). Both the age of Abraham and the age of Sarah yield, using gematria, the number nine and thus the idea of judgment.

And so the question arises, What judgments ought be made in this story concerning the descendants of Abraham? What judgments must be made regarding Ishmael and his descendants? Other judgments ask how so many promises made to Abraham can be fulfilled through one son, Isaac. Many other such queries require judgment, queries that can be triggered by the simple process of including a number in the text that reveals a message.

The Fruits of the Spirit

To a society numerically oriented and symbolically conscious that did not have calculators or scratch paper, the following words of the Apostle Paul have an added message when the fruits are counted. He wrote about being spiritual and listed the outcomes of such a process, outcomes that make judgments. We try to determine whether these judgments apply to us. We see whether they "add up," so to speak, in our lives. Paul may well have affixed a certain number to the qualities in the letter he wrote to the Galatians, when he said:

> The fruit of the Spirit is love, joy, peace, long-suffering, gentleness, goodness, faith, meekness, temperance: against such there is no law. (Galatians 5:22–23)

How many qualities did Paul include as a fruit of the Spirit? Might it be for a reason and not simply by chance that there are nine? What is your judgment?

Nine, Unmentioned Yet Present

Consideration of the significance of numbers is not a simple investigation, noting only when a number is used. Scholars have pined away countless days and years searching for evidence that lies within the written scriptural texts. Those of us who already have the printed texts—fresh off the press, either in book form or even loaded on our searchable computer disks and drives—we may have a difficult time identifying with scribes who copied them assiduously by hand.

Scribes, monks, and priests, who gave careful attention to every letter and mark they made on every text, offer a far different perspective from what we, who read and study for meaning and interpretation, offer. We don't have to make our own copies of the holy writings by hand, with tools that long ago have been discarded. Bible scholars of the past found the following as they

examined and counted:
- Nine warning judgments listed in Haggai 1:11.
- Nine persons afflicted with blindness in the Old Testament.
- Nine persons afflicted with leprosy in the Old Testament.
- Nine persons stoned in the Old and New Testaments combined.

Could these numbers be significant? We are left to make our own judgment.

A Well-Known Nine of Judgment

Although not mentioned in the Bible, the infamous cat-o'-nine-tails may well have its origin in this most revered book. This was an instrument of punishment used and named during the seventeenth century. It was used in the British army and navy for a time and most likely had its beginnings aboard ships, where ropes would be handy. Several ropes are called cats, as in cat harpings, which were used to brace the shrouds; or cat falls, which pass over the cat-head (E. Cobham Brewer, *Brewer's Dictionary*, 223–24).

A cat-o'-nine-tails was made of nine ropes, joined together at a handle or grip. The reason for the multiple tail was to increase the punishment without going beyond the number of stripes prescribed. It was a way to make the punishment match the severity of a crime. Records indicate that each tail could have as many as twenty knots tied into it, as well as fragments of material such as metal or bone. Thus, this device was extremely dreaded as an instrument of judgment.

Conclusion

If we want to know the essence of a symbol, it is wise to look for the manner in which the symbol is used. Examine all instances in which the symbol is mentioned as well as those in which it is applied. Carefully study its nature. Ask, What is unique about it? What can it do that nothing else can do? What can it do better than anything else? Also investigate how others have used the symbol.

This thorough study leads to the best possible concept associated with a symbol. It should also help determine whether the symbol has been or is currently used as such.

Upon examining the number nine in this crucible, under the light shed when answering these questions, the idea of judgment comes forth most strongly associated with this number. Such symbolism can be applied to every time the number nine is used in scriptural texts.

10

The Number That Establishes Perfect Order

The number ten is not a single-digit or simple number. It is the first of a new set of numbers made from multiple numbers. Because of these natural assets of character and position, ten is a prime candidate to be used as a significant symbol.

The number is used enough times in scriptural text that the pattern of its use can be observed and conclusions can be made. The number ten is often used to indicate the total number of people or objects in a parable or event. It communicates order when used in such instances. Reasons for this number being so common and suggesting order comes because every person is equipped with ten toes and ten fingers. We constantly use our fingers as tools by which counts are made and order is established.

The Number of Ordinal Perfection

Because of such inherent characteristics, the number ten has been identified by many scriptural scholars as the number symbolic of ordinal perfection. An ordinal number is defined as one that not only gives a count but also sets an order. The perfection part of the designation possibly has its origin, whether by coincidence or design, in the idea that the number ten is the result of combining the number three and the number seven. The number three, as previously described, suggests fullness. The number seven, also previously described, suggests completeness and perfection. When these two numbers or thoughts combine, a feeling or sense of maximum, the best, the ultimate, or perfection, is a conclusive product.

This combined result and idea can be applied to many parables, events, and descriptions to suggest that all of them are without fault or error, deficit or shortcoming.

Distinction between the symbolic messages of the numbers three, seven, and ten may be difficult at first to identify. However, each has a unique element or message. Their message may parallel that of another, but they are not the same. Identifying and keeping each number separate helps in identifying the messages they send. This can be done when they are used separately or when they are combined. The number three suggests primarily a fullness. The number seven suggests perfection. The number ten suggests an order and an accounting. This ordering and assessment suggests fullness or perfection.

Fingers and Toes

We all know we have ten fingers and ten toes, and that knowledge makes it easy to choose ten as a symbol that is common and well known. Combine this commonality with the idea that the hands with ten fingers and the feet with ten toes have the full capacity to do God's work and go wherever God directs or desires. Now contrast this concept with the description given to the Anakims, from whom Goliath, the giant of David's combat, descended. The contest between David and Goliath occurred in this setting:

> Now the Philistines gathered together their armies to battle, and were gathered together at Shochoh, which belongeth to Judah, and pitched between Shochoh and Azekah, in Ephes-dammim.
> And Saul and the men of Israel were gathered

together, and pitched by the valley of Elah, and set the battle in array against the Philistines.

And the Philistines stood on a mountain on the one side, and Israel stood on a mountain on the other side: and there was a valley between them.

And there went out a champion out of the camp of the Philistines, named Goliath, of Gath, whose height was six cubits and a span.

And he had an helmet of brass upon his head, and he was armed with a coat of mail; and the weight of the coat was five thousand shekels of brass.

And he had greaves of brass upon his legs, and a target of brass between his shoulders.

And the staff of his spear was like a weaver's beam; and his spear's head weighed six hundred shekels of iron: and one bearing a shield went before him.

And he stood and cried unto the armies of Israel, and said unto them, Why are ye come out to set your battle in array? am not I a Philistine, and ye servants to Saul? choose you a man for you, and let him come down to me.

If he be able to fight with me, and to kill me, then will we be your servants: but if I prevail against him, and kill him, then shall ye be our servants, and serve us.

And the Philistine said, I defy the armies of Israel this day; give me a man, that we may fight together.

When Saul and all Israel heard those words of the Philistine, they were dismayed, and greatly afraid. (1 Samuel 17: 1–11)

Under those conditions and against such a terrible foe, David battled Goliath and killed him. Later on, during the campaigns of King David when they were charged with clearing the land of Canaan of enemies, David's warriors were confronted with the brother of Goliath as well as his sons. The account, told in Chronicles, is as follows:

> And there was war again with the Philistines; and Elhanan the son of Jair slew Lahmi the brother of Goliath the Gittite, whose spear staff was like a weaver's beam.
>
> And yet again there was war at Gath, where was a man of great stature, whose fingers and toes were four and twenty, six on each hand, and six on each foot: and he also was the son of the giant.
>
> But when he defied Israel, Jonathan the son of Shimea David's brother slew him.
>
> These were born unto the giant in Gath; and they fell by the hand of David, and by the hand of his servants. (1 Chronicles 20:5–8)

Possibly six fingers was a genetic occurrence or mutation, but should this be considered literal? The scriptures contain other descriptions of Goliath's size as well as measurements of his armaments. Do we take them to be literal? Why are they mentioned in the account? These were marauders to the Israelites. They didn't have ten toes or ten fingers. What is significant about that? Would this provide an advantage over David or the Israelites?

These Philistines who opposed Israel were not following the desires of the God of Israel. They each had twelve fingers and twelve toes, six on each hand and foot. What is the symbolism and message for the number six? As discussed previously, six represents the number of man and the things of man. It often indicates falling short of the desired mark.

The Philistines never attained the desired goal that the Israelites felt God had for them. Could there be a dualistic message in the recorded number of toes and fingers of this giant?

Figurative expressions in our own times describing physical abilities leave questions about what should be taken literally. We say such things as, "I'm all thumbs today." "He eats and drinks sports." "They walked all over their opponents all season long." "He carries the whole team on his broad shoulders." "He was a bushy-tailed, forked-tongued, two-faced fox." "The ball had eyes." "There was a lid on our basket." Or, "He has a fire in his belly."

The list could continue with many more expressions until we go into "sudden death."

In our present culture, we seldom challenge the literary license of writers when they figuratively describe people and events with so much imagery. Should we not give the same license to the authors of scriptural accounts? After all, they are from an Eastern culture, one more prone to produce images not necessarily accurate in detail. To read these Eastern texts with a Western eye and ear causes one to miss much of the message that was intended to reach the heart.

An Accounting—Complete and Full

Returning to the idea of ten representing accounting as well as perfection, we should examine the application of this number to other situations, as well.

God gave ten commandments. Is it significant that there were ten and not nine or eleven? There is not a stronger edict with which we can give an accounting than to apply the ten commandments.

Before Sinai, God's message was given to the Pharaoh and the Egyptian nation. It warned of ten plagues (see Exodus 8–12). Not only were there ten plagues, but the tenth one was truly full and complete, the one that would be undeniable in its effect and power. The tenth plague pointed to the perfect deliverer whom God would send to save all. The Israelites were to kill the paschal lamb and put blood from the lamb upon every doorpost and lintel.

The paschal lamb symbolized God's son, the Messiah, who would come and shed His atoning blood to save all men who were in bondage to sin. The destroying angel would pass over every such marked household. This judgment would be full and complete, and it would come based upon a full accounting of the sins of a nation, that would not recognize the God of heaven and earth. Judgment and punishment, ordinal and lacking nothing, would come against the Egyptian people and their king, who had fettered and abused Israel. There seems sufficient reason for the number ten to be the element of focus in these events.

The parable of the ten virgins distinguishes between those who are prepared for the marriage supper and those who are not. The number ten seems to indicate that it includes everyone. Either we are ready or we are not. The parable of the ten lepers (Luke 17:12–19), of the ten servants and pounds (Luke 19:12–27), and of the ten coins (Luke 15:8, 9), all fall under this same consideration of giving an accounting in our personal lives.

The Ten Tribes

Questions arise when we try to determine why the tribes of the northern kingdom of Israel, originally reigned over by Jeroboam, were numbered as ten. These tribes were taken into bondage by the Assyrians and are referred to as the lost ten tribes of Israel. The rest of Israel's descendants not under Jeroboam's reign lived in the southern kingdom of Judah. Due to the fact that the tribe of Joseph became the tribes of Ephraim and Manasseh, Joseph's sons, there should have been eleven of them, so why are they still called the ten tribes (D&C 110:11; Articles of Faith 1:10)?

The answer to this question lies within this idea of the number ten. Ten suggests the numerical counting of all the tribes that were not a part of the kingdom of Judah, ruled first by Solomon and afterward by his son, Rehoboam. After being snubbed by King Rehoboam, these tribes wanted their own kingdom, apart from Judah.

The prophet Ahijah planted this idea of being a kingdom of ten tribes into the mind of Jeroboam. Ahijah came to Jeroboam because of the sins of Solomon, king of all twelve tribes. Ahijah tore Jeroboam's garment into twelve pieces; then he gave ten of the pieces to Jeroboam. "And he said to Jeroboam, Take thee ten pieces: for thus saith the LORD, the God of Israel, Behold, I will rend the kingdom out of the hand of Solomon, and will give ten tribes to thee" (1 Kings 11:31).

The idea of ten suited those who followed Jeroboam. In their minds, they had no deficit or shortfall as they accounted the virtues of their kingdom and compared them to the apostate kingdom of Judah. They were to be ruled by a king, noted to be, at the time, "a mighty man of valour" (1 Kings 11:28).

The idea of ten fits this group of tribes because they had been judged or accounted. Even when they were taken away into dispersion and separated, they could still be referred to as the ten tribes because they deserved the reward of their disobedience. They had been forewarned, as well as warned, regarding their impending doom if they chose to turn from God's ways and choose the ways of their neighbors. When they were accounted and assessed as transgressors, they could rightly be given the designation of ten.

Nebuchadnezzar's Vision

The feet and toes of the image in Nebuchadnezzar's vision (Daniel 2) can be interpreted in this same light. Nebuchadnezzar saw a vision in which he beheld a terrible image. The head of the image was of gold. The breast and the arms were silver. The belly and thighs were brass. The legs were iron. Last to be mentioned were the feet, which were part iron and part clay.

We read in the text of Daniel that the toes represent kingdoms that will come into future existence:

> And whereas thou sawest the feet and toes, part of potters' clay, and part of iron, the kingdom shall be divided; but there shall be in it of the strength of the iron, forasmuch as thou sawest the iron mixed with miry clay.
>
> And as the toes of the feet were part of iron, and part of clay, so the kingdom shall be partly strong, and partly broken.
>
> And whereas thou sawest iron mixed with miry clay, they shall mingle themselves with the seed of

men: but they shall not cleave one to another, even as iron is not mixed with clay.

And in the days of these kings shall the God of heaven set up a kingdom, which shall never be destroyed: and the kingdom shall not be left to other people, but it shall break in pieces and consume all these kingdoms, and it shall stand for ever.

Forasmuch as thou sawest that the stone was cut out of the mountain without hands, and that it brake in pieces the iron, the brass, the clay, the silver, and the gold; the great God hath made known to the king what shall come to pass hereafter: and the dream is certain, and the interpretation thereof sure. (Daniel 2:41–45)

Notice that the text does not mention the number ten. However, the number may naturally come to the reader's mind. Of course the feet would have ten toes, which possibly suggests ten kingdoms that would one day be broken in pieces. Ten gives the idea of ordinal perfection, suggesting an accounting to see if anything is lacking. These kingdoms would be broken into pieces by the stone cut out of the mountain. They would be found wanting and worthy of replacement by this new kingdom, which would stand forever. That new kingdom would be the kingdom of God.

Other Accountings

When determining the fate and future of the cities of Sodom and Gomorrah, Abraham sues God for sparing the cities (Genesis 18). The Lord agrees to this plan if Abraham can find a certain number of righteous individuals. How many? Ten! Is it possible that this number expresses the idea that there took place a great accounting?

Back to the story of Jacob, who married four wives when he was away from his own parents and twin brother. When Jacob rehearsed how many times Laban, his father-in-law, had changed his wages, he gave the number ten (Genesis 31:7). The story does not give the details of Jacob's wages being changed. However, one gets the idea from reading the words of Jacob that this was an actual fact and that there was an injustice done to him by Laban, the father to two of his wives.

Having considered in previous chapters the numbers two, six, and seven, with their symbolic messages, it is interesting to reread Jacob's words to Laban. He said, "Thus have I been twenty years in thy house; I served thee fourteen years for thy two daughters, and six years for thy cattle: and thou hast changed my wages ten times" (Genesis 31:41).

Should these numbers be taken as literal or symbolic? Some may want to read them as exactly what they say in terms or years or times. But bear in mind the culture in which Jacob and Laban were living. Also consider that this was an emotionally charged meeting. This was not just an employer from whom Jacob was taking leave; this was his father-in-law.

Jacob was also leaving his employ. He was taking with him a good deal of wealth, to which he felt he was entitled. Finally, he was taking away Laban's daughters and grandchildren. To justify such a situation, graphic, impassioned expressions were needed. Jacob needed to go beyond the literal words and communicate feelings to Laban's mind and heart. So he tells Laban that he had been twenty years in his house.

Twenty is assigned to the Hebrew letter *Kaf*, the twentieth letter in their index. As with all the other letters and numbers, a symbol and message belong to it. The message of number twenty concerns toiling, labor, and the power to rule. Remember, the record says that Joseph was sold by his brothers into slavery for twenty pieces of silver (Genesis 37:28). This was also the age at which one would become a soldier or pursue a livelihood.

Fourteen is *two* (witness) times *seven* (perfection, nothing lacking) in regard to Laban's *two* daughters and his relationship with them—not just one daughter but *two* (witness), both Rachel and Leah. No mention is made of his other two wives, called handmaidens, whose children would also be accounted as Laban's. Jacob used the number *two* in his plea for understanding to suggest that this was not his thinking alone. Others had witnessed it. There was not just one daughter and wife but two.

The use of the number *six* (things of man) divides Jacob's devotion to Laban from his serving him for his daughters. Seven was reflective of perfection. Six is the number used when assessing earthly possessions or traits of the flesh.

Ten (accounted and measured) is the number of times Jacob's wages had been changed during fits of Laban's anger. Whether you apply the literal or figurative idea of the number, Jacob seems fully justified in leaving.

Jacob's expressions to Laban are reminiscent of a love letter received by a sweetheart who was trying to hold on to the love she had for her boyfriend who was away attending school. In his letter, he wrote, "My love. For you I'd swim the widest river, I'd climb the highest mountain. I'd walk a thousand miles just to be by your side." Then he closed his dispatch by writing, "I'll be home this weekend—if it doesn't storm."

When the sweetheart received the letter, surely she had to decipher which statements were literal and which were figurative. She probably also wondered why he said some of those things if a single weekend storm would keep him away. So was the message of Jacob literal or figurative?

Allowing Jacob some figurative terminology in his reply to his father-in-law seems appropriate. He paints a picture that is accurate to a degree. Its details are less important than the message that is being given. Such is the manner of symbolism.

Tithing

The subject of tithing should be mentioned here. The word *tithe* in modern English originates from the old English word *tien* and *teothung* (*Webster's Dictionary*); both roots contain the concept of ten. The Hebrew word for tithing, *asirit*, itself means one tenth, and the Israelites paid one-tenth of their yearly increase to the tribe of Levi, the priests (Leviticus 27:30–33).

To the Saints of these latter-days the Lord has made clear what He desires. "Those who have thus been tithed shall pay one-tenth of all their interest annually; and this shall be a standing law unto them forever" (D&C 119:4). There is little question, after that declaration by the Lord, about what currently constitutes a tithe.

However, because the number ten is within the root of the word tithe, giving such an offering is more than just donating 10 percent. It suggests that there should be an order and an accounting. What should one really give?

President David O. McKay told of how his father had molded his life in regard to tithing. He said that he and his brother were hauling hay from their fields during the years when tithes were paid in kind. President McKay said he and his brother had driven to the field to get the tenth load of hay and were headed back to the part of the meadow from where they had taken the ninth load. In that field there was wire grass and slough grass. As they began to load the hay, their father called for them to leave that field and go up to higher ground, where their better hay grew. Their father told them that the best is none too good for God (*Cherished Experiences from the Writings of President David O. McKay*, 20).

Other tithing stories record the best animals or other products being given as payment of tithes. The number ten can suggest to both the mind and the heart that an offering should not be measured simply by the amount. The spirit of the number ten can help when determining how we should feel about our offerings. And how we feel may have an effect on the quality as well as the amount that should be given.

Dimensions, Measurements, and Details

The number ten is the prevailing figure in the dimensions and measurements of the tabernacle built during the exodus (Exodus 26:1, 16; 27:12, the temple of Solomon (1 Kings 6:26; 27:23, 24, 27, 37, 38, 49), the temple of Ezekiel's vision (Ezekiel

40:11; 41:2; 42:4). We also notice that it is not just the number ten that appears so often but multiples of the number ten as well. The number ten is used to give the lengths of materials, widths of objects, numbers of objects, and amounts of incense, oil, and offerings too numerous to list.

The number ten also details how many curtains, pillars, bases, knops, and loaves are to be used or placed in the worship places. The molten sea described in 1 Kings 7:23–24 was ten cubits in diameter, with knops under the brim round about numbering ten knops in each cubit length.

The numbers four and five likewise consistently appear describing dimensions and counts. Their symbolic messages stand alongside the number ten within these structures and objects. To the minds of those who built or assembled such structures, as well as all who would enter therein, there could come the powerful message of order and accounting if they were aware of the symbolism of the number ten.

The Number Ten Used by the Apostle John

I hope we have established that scriptural texts contain more imagery than at first meets the eye. If so, we might move beyond simply the use of the word ten and see if authors may have counted the number of times they listed significant elements. Possible emphasis of accounting, completeness, fullness, and perfection would be the result of such detail.

Consider what the Apostle John put in his gospel. In his testimony, he seems to be trying to prove, in a prophetic and allegorical manner, that Jesus was the promised Messiah. The name "I am," though not always translated in that correct form, was a significant title of Jehovah. The Messiah would be Jehovah, come in the flesh. Through a careful reading and accounting of John's marvelous record, we can find ten declarations by John that contain the name or declaration of "I am."

"I am the bread of life" (6:35).

"I am the bread of life which came down from heaven" (6:41).

"I am the living bread" (6:51).

"I am the light of the world" (8:12).

"I am one that bear witness of myself" (8:18).

"I am the door of the sheepfold" (10:7, 9).

"I am the good shepherd" (10:14).

"I am the resurrection and the life" (11:25).

"I am the way, the truth, and the life" (14:6).

"I am the true vine" (15:1, 5).

Each of these statements should make us evaluate and assess. We could ask, "Do I believe that Christ is the living water or the good shepherd?" Our answer is powerful and introspective.

However, if we become aware that John included ten of these statements that incite accounting and assessment, that message can be amplified to a degree that surely would be even more moving to the soul. Such impact is based upon knowing the literary significance and symbolism of the number ten.

The Number Ten Used by the Apostle Paul

The Apostle Paul also uses this same literary tool. In his letter to the Roman Saints, Paul sent a list of seven things that could separate them from the love of Christ. (We recognize the symbolic power of seven, which has been identified as the idea of perfection).

He presents his list in the form of a question: "Who shall separate us from the love of Christ? Shall [1] tribulation, or [2] distress, or [3] persecution, or [4] famine, or [5] nakedness, or [6] peril, or [7] sword?" (Romans 8:35).

Does the list have more effect because Paul included seven elements? To some it may not, but to others it may.

Paul then continues, "For I am persuaded, that neither [1] death, nor [2] life, nor [3] angels, nor [4] principalities, nor [5] powers, nor [6] things present, nor [7] things to come, nor [8]

138—Unlocking the Numbers

height, nor [9] depth, nor any [10] other creature, shall be able to separate us from the love of God, which is in Christ Jesus our Lord" (Romans 8:38–39).

What is he saying when he incorporates a list of ten things? Perhaps he is saying that the things he listed cannot separate us from God's love, and that his list is complete. In other words, there is absolutely nothing that can separate us from the love of God!

Paul likewise listed elements in his letter to the Hebrews that surely were significant to them. He told the Hebrews that they belonged to the Church of the Firstborn and that they had moved beyond being troubled and therefore defiled. He wrote, "But ye are come unto mount [1] Sion, and unto the [2] city of the living God, the [3] heavenly Jerusalem, and to [4] an innumerable company of angels, To the [5] general assembly and [6] church of the first born, which are written in heaven, and to [7] God the Judge of all, and to the [8] spirits of just men made perfect. And to [9] Jesus the mediator of the new covenant, and to the [10] blood of sprinkling, that speaketh better things than that of Abel" (Hebrews 12:22–24).

The Jewish community received Paul's epistle written to the Hebrews. But he used the same pattern when he wrote to the church members in the Greek city of Corinth. He gives an exhaustive list of disqualifications that would keep them out of God's kingdom: "Know ye not that the unrighteous shall not inherit the kingdom of God? Be not deceived; [1] neither fornicators, [2] nor idolaters, [3] nor adulterers, [4] nor effeminate, [5] nor abusers of themselves with mankind, [6] nor thieves, [7] nor covetous, [8] nor drunkards, [9] nor revilers, [10] nor extortioners, shall inherit the kingdom of God" (1 Corinthians 6:9–10).

Staying with the same subject concerning those who will inherit God's glory, the apostle John wrote:

> And I saw a new heaven and a new earth: for the first heaven and the first earth were passed away; and there was no more sea.

And I John saw the holy city, new Jerusalem, coming down from God out of heaven, prepared as a bride adorned for her husband.

And I heard a great voice out of heaven saying, Behold, the tabernacle of God is with men, and [1] *he will dwell* with them, and they shall [2] *be his people*, and God himself [3] *shall be with them*, and [4] *be their God*.

And God shall [5] *wipe away all tears* from their eyes; and there shall be [6] *no more death*, neither [7] *sorrow*, nor [8] *crying*, neither shall there be any more [9] *pain*: for the [10] *former things* are passed away.

And he that sat upon the throne said, Behold, I make all things new. And he said unto me, Write: for these words are true and faithful.

And he said unto me, It is done. I am Alpha and Omega, the beginning and the end. I will give unto him that is athirst of the fountain of the water of life freely.

He that overcometh shall inherit all things; and I will be his God, and he shall be my son. (Revelation 21:1–7; emphasis added)

In a latter-day revelation, while giving answers and instruction to Joseph Smith Sr. regarding his desires to perform missionary work, the Lord said:

And faith, hope, charity and love, with an eye single to the glory of God, qualify him for the work.

Remember faith, virtue, knowledge, temperance, patience, brotherly kindness, godliness, charity, humility, diligence. (D&C 4:5–6)

Count and note the four elements in verse 5 that qualify one for the work. They must be supplementary to an eye single to the glory of God. The number four suggests how we are qualified to take the gospel to everyone, no matter where, to every nation, kindred, tongue, and people. The idea of four is universality.

The use of ten items appears in the instructions to Joseph Smith Sr. in verse 6. God observed that there were traits that should be remembered. Count these traits. Are we surprised that they number ten? In the writings of three apostles—Joseph Smith, John, and Paul—we find patterns that suggest accounting.

Some may choose to call these mere coincidence. Others may choose to see these listings and descriptions as markers of significance. That is a decision that must be made with all such communication. But symbols enhance and enrich. To some, the sun simply goes down. Others see a beautiful sunset.

Detecting the Number Ten in the Book of Mormon

John W. Welch concluded an article entitled *Counting to Ten*, with these words: "Detecting these tenfold occurrences in the Book of Mormon uncovers a previously unnoticed ancient quality of Nephite scripture that was probably more obvious to ancient minds than it is to modern readers" (*Journal of Book of Mormon Studies* 12 [2 November 2003], 43–57).

His conclusions rise from discoveries of a series of tens previously unnoted in Book of Mormon texts. Prominent among these writings are the ten woes listed by Jacob (see 2 Nephi 9:27, 30–38), the tenfold call to repentance recorded in 3 Nephi 30:2, and the ten uses of sacred names of deity included by King Benjamin in his discourse that seems designed to invite his people to baptism (Mosiah 3:5, 13, 14, 17, 18, 21, 23; compare Mosiah 2:30, 41; 5:15).

Welch also points out dual tens in the beautiful psalm in 2 Nephi 4, wherein the word *Lord* appears ten times, as does the interjection of the word or letter *O*. These uses of the symbolic ten are consistent with the evaluating process of accounting and ordering of our lives and worthiness to participate in covenants or enter the presence of God. Welch relates the number ten to consecration and sacrifice, testing and trials, penitence and atonement, as well as supplication and prayer. His discoveries are stimulating and refreshing. His assessments are scholarly and much appreciated.

The Seventy

Last in this category, a question seems in order. What might come to mind if the idea of spiritual perfection is multiplied by the idea of ordinal perfection? That would be a state, work, or condition that would be holy above all else, an essence upon which God's eye and pleasure would find homage. It would be divine and above and beyond things bound with worldliness. What symbolic numbers could create such a result? It would be the number seven multiplied by the number ten—seventy.

The number seventy appears many times in the scriptures, with a goodly portion of those instances clearly having a literal use. However, some should surely be considered symbolic, including the "seventy elders of Israel" in the days of Moses (see Exodus 24:9) and the seven who were called to serve in the New Testament church (see Acts 6:5). Because clear understanding of the work of the seventy has little consensus among Bible students, a definition of the labors of the seventy as outlined in latter-day scriptures seems significant. The Lord directed:

> The Seventy are also called to preach the gospel, and to be especial witnesses unto the Gentiles and in all the world—thus differing from other officers in the church in the duties of their calling. (D&C 107:25)

> The Seventy are to act in the name of the Lord, under the direction of the Twelve or the traveling high council, in building up the church and regulating all the affairs of the same in all nations, first unto the Gentiles and then to the Jews. (D&C 107:34)

> And it is according to the vision showing the order of the Seventy that they should have seven presidents

to preside over them, chosen out of the number of the seventy. (D&C 107:93)

> These seven presidents are to choose other seventy besides the first seventy to whom they belong, and are to preside over them; and also other seventy, until seven times seventy, if the labor in the vineyard of necessity requires it. And these seventy are to be traveling ministers, unto the Gentiles first and also unto the Jews. (D&C 107:95–97)

These seventy act under the direction of the Twelve Apostles in the work commissioned to them. They are constantly engaged in proclaiming the gospel and perfecting the Saints (D&C 107:34). How fitting are such assignments for quorums, fully given, that bear the name of seven times ten!

Summary and Conclusions

In present-day expressions and evaluations, it doesn't take much to communicate to others that something or someone has been measured and found ideal or exemplary. It takes only the use of one symbolic term—"She's a ten!" or "I give it a ten!" Nothing else needs to be said. The message is understood by all who have any experience regarding assessing people or things.

Contrast the idea of a ten with the idea of "We're number one!" The subtle difference between the two expressions can be noticed if the messages of the two symbolic numbers are compared. The message of the number one is exclusion; the message of the number ten is things assessed and in their proper order. The number one says that something or someone is all alone at the top; the number ten says that when surrounded by all the candidates, all have been assessed completely and they have been put in order. Much like a beauty pageant, ten finalists are selected. They are the top ten. They have been assessed and measured. But then one of the ten is chosen as the queen, excluded from all others.

11

The Number That Is Least Used

The instances wherein the number eleven appears in the scriptures are comparatively few. That would not be so much of an issue if the times it does appear showed more harmony in the manner in which it is used. There appears to be little evidence of writers using this number as a symbol. The following gives a summary of the number eleven as it appears in the scriptures:

The number eleven appears twenty-six times, and these instances can be put into the following categories:

The number eleven appears seven times when referring to the quorum of the apostles, which had eleven members due to the death of Judas Iscariot. Judas took his own life after betraying Jesus.

The number eleven appears five times in verses that tell how old a king was when he began his reign. This may well be an indication that the king was approaching the number twelve, which will be shown later as the number of divine government. To be eleven rather than twelve may thus have been symbolic. Those who ruled at age eleven failed and were not able to rule with the strength and wisdom that would be according to the will of God.

The number eleven is used five more times to give dimensions of places of worship.

Three times the number eleven is used as a ransom price.

The remaining six uses of the number eleven are found, once

each, in these categories: to describe the number of individuals in a village, the number of members of a family, the age when a child was taken with the family to a different land, how far a group traveled in a day's journey, the number of bullocks used in an offering, and the eleven stars that gave obeisance to Joseph's star.

Other than the possible idea that eleven had not reached the number twelve, no other idea for symbolism seems likely. Little comment relative to the number eleven has been generated by writers, who have taken up the cause of identifying other numbers as symbols. Latter-day scripture adds nothing obvious to what the Bible says in regard to the number eleven.

12

The Number That Denotes Divine Government

A consensus of opinion by Bible scholars regarding the symbolic use of the number twelve is nearly unanimous. Nearly every written opinion registers the number twelve as the number for divine government (see Bullinger, *Number in Scripture;* Fairbairn, *The Teachers and Students Bible Encyclopedia;* Unger, *Unger's Concise Bible Dictionary;* Smith, *Smith's Bible Dictionary*). Some of the most influential examples that contribute to this concept are the twelve tribes of Israel, the twelve stones upon the breastplate, and the twelve apostles of the New Testament church.

Priesthood is the Lord's word of choice to identify divine government. Priesthood always has its work and functions based upon the perspective that the gospel work is for every soul, no matter when or where one lives. Priesthood administers the doctrines and ordinances of the gospel, and when the gospel is delivered, it must be full and not just a portion of the power and precepts of its message.

The Number Twelve Indicates Priesthood

The reasons for association between the priesthood and the number twelve seem best to come from determining the factors of the number twelve. These numerical factors can lead to the ideas of priesthood or divine government. Concurrence is universal in selecting the number three and the number four as being the factors of the number twelve. When these two numbers are multiplied, they, of course, result in the number twelve, which is symbolic of priesthood or divine government.

This symbolic result doesn't come because two numbers just happen to be twelve. It comes as the result of multiplying the symbolic message of the number three, the idea of fullness, with the symbolic message of the number four, the idea of universality. Multiplication of the connotation of these two numbers gives a broader and deeper dimension to the result or outcome than either of the numbers does by itself.

An illustration of combining the two messages could be given this way: the apostles were told to go to every (1) nation, (2) kindred, (3) tongue, and (4) people. The number suggests universality, with no one or nothing left out. Combined with the idea of three, they would go *with fullness* to every nation, kindred, tongue, and people.

What is the difference? Some men simply say, "Will you marry me?" Others say, "Will you marry me because I love you and my life is wonderful when I am with you?" Such is the added dimension associated with the symbolic message for the number twelve.

The New Jerusalem

Priesthood, or divine government, can be identified by simple reference or use of the number twelve. John the Revelator described the New Jerusalem, using the number twelve extensively. He wrote:

> And he carried me away in the spirit to a great
> and high mountain, and shewed me that great city, the
> holy Jerusalem, descending out of heaven from God,
> Having the glory of God: and her light was like
> unto a stone most precious, even like a jasper stone,

clear as crystal;

And had a wall great and high, and had *twelve gates*, and at the gates *twelve angels*, and names written thereon, which are the names of the *twelve tribes* of the children of Israel:

On the east three gates; on the north three gates; on the south three gates; and on the west three gates.

And the wall of the city had *twelve foundations*, and in them the names of the *twelve apostles* of the Lamb.

And he that talked with me had a golden reed to measure the city, and the gates thereof, and the wall thereof.

And the city lieth foursquare, and the length is as large as the breadth: and he measured the city with the reed, *twelve thousand* furlongs. The length and the breadth and the height of it are equal.

And he measured the wall thereof, an hundred and forty and four cubits, according to the measure of a man, that is, of the angel.

And the building of the wall of it was of jasper: and the city was pure gold, like unto clear glass.

And the foundations of the wall of the city were garnished with all manner of precious stones. The first foundation was jasper; the second, sapphire; the third, a chalcedony; the fourth, an emerald;

The fifth, sardonyx; the sixth, sardius; the seventh, chrysolite; the eighth, beryl; the ninth, a topaz; the tenth, a chrysoprasus; the eleventh, a jacinth; the twelfth, an amethyst.

And the twelve gates were *twelve pearls;* every several gate was of one pearl: and the street of the city was pure gold, as it were transparent glass.

And I saw no temple therein: for the Lord God Almighty and the Lamb are the temple of it. (Revelation 21:10–22; emphasis added)

Not only did John use the number twelve, but he also used the numbers three and four, with varying forms of those numbers, in his description of the Holy City. The idea of divine government, or priesthood, is represented upon every feature of the city. Furthermore, everyone who reads his account is intended to feel that the government of this city will not be corrupt, for God will be there and His rule will be everywhere and full.

We can observe the symbolic number of twelve not just in the design of the holy city but also in existing temples. The Salt Lake Temple has three spires on the east and three on the west. The three spires on the east are six feet higher than those on the west, and they represent the presidency of the Melchizedek Priesthood. The three spires on the west represent the presidency of the Aaronic Priesthood.

On each of these spires are twelve pinnacles. Truman O. Angell, architect of the Salt Lake Temple, wrote, "Each tower has a spire and 12 pinnacles which are representative of the First Presidency, the Twelve Apostles, and the high council" (*Millennial Star* 36 [5 May 1874], 273–75). Knowing the symbolic significance of numbers makes it difficult to view the Salt Lake Temple without being awestruck.

However, the idea of twelve as a symbol is on display inside each and every temple. The baptismal font in each temple is placed upon the backs of oxen. The symbolic message is that the work that goes on within the font rests upon the back, or shoulders, of the oxen. That is where burdens are symbolically, as well as literally, placed.

And what do the oxen represent? The tribe of Ephraim, as well as his brethren, the other sons of Israel. Ephraim is to lead in the labor that goes on in the fonts, and his symbol is that of a bullock with horns (Deuteronomy 33:17). And how many oxen are under each baptismal font? Twelve. There should be twelve if the work that goes on there has to do with divine government or priesthood.

The Twelve Shall Judge

The priesthood will not just rule, it will also judge. Jesus responded to Peter and the rest of the apostles with this declaration: "Ye also shall sit upon twelve thrones, judging the twelve tribes of Israel" (Matthew 19:28).

The prophet Nephi was given similar but additional instructions as to how the judgment of Israel would take place. Nephi recorded what was told to him by an angel:

> And he said unto me: Thou rememberest the twelve apostles of the Lamb? Behold they are they who shall judge the twelve tribes of Israel; wherefore, the twelve ministers of thy seed shall be judged of them; for ye are of the house of Israel.
>
> And these twelve ministers whom thou beholdest shall judge thy seed. And, behold, they are righteous forever; for because of their faith in the Lamb of God their garments are made white in his blood. (1 Nephi 12:9–10)

From the vision given to Nephi by the angel, we ascertain the following:

- The Lamb would have twelve apostles in His ministry in Jerusalem.
- The Lamb would also have twelve other ministers (apostles) from among the seed of Lehi.
- The twelve of Jerusalem would judge the house of Israel.
- The twelve of Jerusalem would judge the twelve of Lehi.
- The twelve of Lehi would judge the seed of Lehi.

In 1830, the Lord said to the Prophet Joseph Smith:

> And again, verily, verily, I say unto you, and it hath

> gone forth in a firm decree, by the will of the Father, that mine apostles, the Twelve which were with me in my ministry at Jerusalem, shall stand at my right hand at the day of my coming in a pillar of fire, being clothed with robes of righteousness, with crowns upon their heads, in glory even as I am, to judge the whole house of Israel, even as many as have loved me and kept my commandments, and none else. (D&C 29:12)

These declarations only speak of the twelve, not the fifteen, thirteen, or the twenty-one members of a quorum. This is because of the symbolism possessed by the number twelve, which signifies divine priesthood government. This symbolism attempts to communicate to the observer not how many will judge as much as it describes the judgment itself. It indicates that the judgment will be divine and under God's control. It suggests that the judgment will consider things fully. And it also denotes that there will not be anyone or anything that will not be brought to a proper judgment. Those are the ideas projected by twelve judges, a message communicated by combining and multiplying the significant, and symbolic numbers three and four.

Twelve Is Everywhere in Priesthood

The offices of the priesthood lack definition as they are mentioned in the text of the Bible. However, revelations in the Doctrine and Covenants change that. In 1835, the Lord instructed:

> And again, verily I say unto you, the duty of a president over the office of a deacon is to preside over *twelve deacons*, to sit in council with them, and to teach them their duty, edifying one another, as it is given according to the covenants.
>
> And also the duty of the president over the office of the teachers is to preside over *twenty-four of the teachers*, and to sit in council with them, teaching them the duties of their office, as given in the covenants.

> Also the duty of the president over the Priesthood
> of Aaron is to preside over *forty-eight priests*, and sit in
> council with them, to teach them the duties of their
> office, as is given in the covenants—
> This president is to be a bishop; for this is one of
> the duties of this priesthood.
> Again, the duty of the president over the office of
> elders is to preside over *ninety-six elders*, and to sit in
> council with them, and to teach them according to the
> covenants. (D&C 107:85–89; emphasis added)

Wards are generally organized in such a manner that each ward contains one quorum of deacons, one of teachers, one of priests, and one of elders. In practicality, these numbers do not match very well the number of members that exist within most wards. The first three quorums belong to the Aaronic Priesthood, and they would, in most situations, operate best if the numbers of twelve, twenty-four, and forty-eight could be reversed.

The reason for this suggestion is that, nearly always, the number of deacons would be closer to the number forty-eight than to the number twelve. In like fashion, the number of priests would be closer to twelve than to forty-eight. This supports the concept that the number twelve is a symbol. It suggests that the number specified is not as significant as the symbolism that it projects. The numbers for the quorums are all multiples of twelve. Even the ninety-six, which is the number of elders who are to be in each quorum, is eight (mercy) times twelve. The message of every one of these numbers is priesthood or divine government!

Other twelves that should be considered with this concept of priesthood include the twelve stones of Elijah's altar 1 Kings 18:31, 32); the twelve jewels in the high priest's breastplate (Exodus 28:21); the twelve cakes of shewbread (Leviticus 24:5); the twelve pillars set up by Moses (Exodus 24:4); and the twelve spies sent to the land of Canaan (Numbers 13). Note also the twelve stones placed in the bed of the Jordan River (Joshua 4:9) and the twelve officers Solomon appointed (1 Kings 4:7)

Taking Twelve to the Limit

The number twelve has been examined and been found to be a magnificent messenger of fullness and totality. Now, let the message of the number twelve be multiplied by the number twelve, in other words, to square it. What would be the result? It should be beyond description! It would be beyond temporal, fuller than full, a cup that runs over. It would be beyond boundaries, "forever and ever," and "worlds without number." That is the message of one hundred and forty four!

Now, moving figuratively beyond that, there is one idea that God and His prophets have used to try and communicate the reward of the righteous. The idea is to amplify a number by multiplying it by one hundred or one thousand. To multiply by "an hundred fold" is significant (Matthew 19:29), but to multiply a number by a thousand, especially after it has been squared (Draper, 83). That idea is beyond description!

In such a case, expressions come to mind such as "Eye hath not seen, nor ear heard, neither have entered into the heart of man, the things which God hath prepared for them that love him" (1 Corinthians 2:9). Another is "Thrones, kingdoms, principalities, and powers, dominions, all heights and depths . . . and they shall pass by the angels, and the gods, which are set there, to their exaltation and glory in all things, as hath been sealed upon their heads, which glory shall be a fulness and a continuation of the seeds forever and ever" (D&C 132:19). That is the idea of one hundred and forty four thousand.

Some of the uses of this squared, amplified number are as follows:

> And I looked, and, lo, a Lamb stood on the mount Sion, and with him an hundred forty and four thousand, having his Father's name written in their foreheads.
>
> And they sung as it were a new song before the throne, and before the four beasts, and the elders: and no man could learn that song but the hundred and

forty and four thousand, which were redeemed from
the earth. (Revelation 14:1, 3)

Q. What are we to understand by sealing the one
hundred and forty–four thousand, out of all the tribes
of Israel—twelve thousand out of every tribe?

A. We are to understand that those who are sealed
are high priests, ordained unto the holy order of God,
to administer the everlasting gospel; for they are they
who are ordained out of every nation, kindred, tongue,
and people, by the angels to whom is given power over
the nations of the earth, to bring as many as will come
to the church of the Firstborn. (D&C 77:11)

Is Heaven Limited to 144,000?

The question comes to mind, Will only those who enjoy this
reward be part of a literal one hundred and forty-four thousand?
Will there be room for me? Surely this question must be answered
with the same consideration given the message of the number
twelve and the other numbers.

This consideration is that the message is greater than the
numerical value. There have been sufficient numbers of leaders
in the past, as well as those currently living, to fill the quota of
one hundred and forty-four thousand. So one might ask if there
is still a chance to be one of this number. Of course there will be
room for all who qualify. The number is not necessarily literal; it
has a message.

Another question arises in regard to having the Father's name
being written upon the forehead. The entire message of the above
verses is figurative and should be considered such. God's law is
written on our hearts (2 Nephi 8:7), and our names are engraven
upon the palms of God's hands (Isaiah 49:16). Should we consider these things literal? To do so detracts from the powerful

symbolism that has been considered. To be one of the hundred and forty-four thousand with the reward that has been discussed, no outward label or mark will be needed. God has already marked everyone so qualified.

13

The Number That Is Most Misunderstood

The number forty is used so frequently within the scriptures that we should definitely evaluate whether it has a symbolic message associated with it. But with a Western mind and Western logic, the question is still asked, Does the number forty mean thirty-nine plus one, or is there a connotation or emphasis that is more important than the exact number of years, days, or cubits mentioned?" Possibly a dualistic meaning—that the number is literal as well as figurative—should be considered. However, this question should not be answered until we have heard from those who have studied long and hard the application and use of the number forty.

Regarding this number, one scholarly group concluded: "This number has been used to symbolically communicate the themes of punishment, affliction, preparation, and cleansing" (*Teachers and Students' Bible Encyclopedia*, 5:38).

Forty Symbolizes Punishment, Affliction, Preparation, and Cleansing

When the idea of the number forty being a symbol of punishment and cleansing is applied, notice the emphasis or message felt by reading the several scriptural references: "And God told Noah: For yet seven days, and I will cause it to rain upon the earth forty days and forty nights; and every living substance that I have made will I destroy from off the face of the earth" (Genesis 7:4).

The water was to cleanse the earth because "the wickedness of men had become great in the earth; and every man was lifted up in the imagination of the thoughts of his heart, being only evil continually" (Moses 8:22).

Not only did it rain upon the earth for forty days and nights, but the waters also increased after that and bare up the ark (see Genesis 7:17). So the question follows: Why does the record in the Bible tell us that it flooded for forty days when that was not the end of the rain? That same question applies when we read the verse that tells us that the waters prevailed longer than the forty days. It reads, "And the waters prevailed upon the earth an hundred and fifty days" (Genesis 7:24).

When it came time to open the window of the ark, the account uses the number forty again. After so much suffering and hardship for the whole earth, and for everyone and everything on board the ark, what a time to suggest more cleansing! Yet, Genesis 8:6 reads, "And it came to pass at the end of forty days, that Noah opened the window of the ark which he had made."

The word *quarantine* can be considered here. Of course, the word has the sense of four. It also has the sense of forty, which is ten times four. Throughout history, when a ship was suspected of carrying a contagious disease, it was forbidden all intercourse with the shore. It was quarantined. And the time for the cleansing and purification of the ship was generally forty days (see *Webster's Dictionary*, 1961).

It is interesting to examine how many times certain numbers are used in the scriptural records. For example, notice how many times the number forty is used as opposed to how seldom other numbers such as thirty-eight, thirty-nine, and forty-one are used.

In all of the combined scriptural texts, or the Standard Works, the following numbers appear in this frequency:

- Thirty-eight, thirty and eight, thirty and eighth":
  six times

- Thirty-nine, thirty and nine, thirty and ninth:
  four times

- Forty: 121 times

- Forty-one, forty and one, forty and first: three
  times

The number of times the number forty is used, compared to surrounding numbers, must raise the question of why. Why was it used so often to indicate the number of days, years, or people? If there were literal counts being taken, why would it so often result in being the number of forty rather than some other number?

Another question that presents itself is, Am I not to believe what the scripture says? It says forty. Why should I think it means anything besides thirty-nine plus one?"

Understanding the idea that Eastern people are much more like artists than Western people should help with the answer. Eastern writers are not nearly so interested in being accurate in all the details as they are in projecting an image that offers feeling and emotion. Compared to Western writers who are more like architects and want to make every detail fit and be exact, Eastern writers are more likely to use figurative symbols that reflect ideas rather than literal descriptions that simply provide facts. The Bible was written by Eastern people for Eastern readers.

As the account of Noah and the great flood is considered, the most powerful message in the account must be relative to God showing His displeasure at the disobedience of His children. Consequently, He is cleansing His creations that they may accomplish their divine purpose. The cleansing may have been for forty years or days, but if that number was a symbol, then we must remember that the number is not as important as what it represents.

Moses' Work Described by Forty

Notice the use of the following scriptures as they convey the message of preparation as well as punishment and cleansing:

> And Moses went into the midst of the cloud, and gat him up into the mount: and Moses was in the mount forty days and forty nights. (Exodus 24:18)

> And he was there with the Lord forty days and forty nights; he did neither eat bread, nor drink water. And he wrote upon the tables the words of the covenant, the ten commandments. (Exodus 34:28)

> When I was gone up into the mount to receive the tables of stone, [even] the tables of the covenant which the Lord made with you, then I abode in the mount forty days and forty nights, I neither did eat bread nor drink water. (Deuteronomy 9:9)

> And I fell down before the Lord, as at the first, forty days and forty nights: I did neither eat bread, nor drink water, because of all your sins which ye sinned, in doing wickedly in the sight of the Lord, to provoke him to anger. (Deuteronomy 9:18)

Moses' Life Described by Forty

Deuteronomy 34:7 tells us that Moses lived till he was a hundred and twenty years of age. Combining that knowledge with Exodus 7:7 and Acts 7:23, 30, the conclusion has long ago been made that Moses' life was divided into three forty-year periods. Does this seems convenient—or coincidental? As the account of his life is read, everything he does seems to take forty days or forty years.

The first period in Moses' life was when he was a prince in

Egypt. This was a critical preparation for when he would later stand before Pharaoh and demand to let this people go. Therefore, it is written as forty years (see Acts 7:23).

The second period of his life took place in the wilderness under the tutelage of his father-in-law, Jethro, the priest of Midian. This was his preparation for becoming a prophet (see Acts 7:30).

The third portion of Moses' life was spent with the Israelites while they prepared themselves to enter the promised land (see Acts 7:36, 42). Even though Moses didn't enter the land, he was prepared and did see it.

Moses' mission extended beyond his mortal life, for he did not die. (Peterson, *Moses, Man of Miracles*, 184–85). He simply moved on to other work he had been prepared to do. We learn from the writings of the prophet Alma that Moses did not taste of death (Alma 45:19), and we know from latter-day revelation that Moses has been in charge of work that has extended beyond his mortal life (D&C 110:11). Little wonder that Moses' life is described the way it is! For all that he did, he had to be prepared.

Forty and the Death of Jacob

Another possible illustration of preparation occurs when Jacob, or Israel, died. He made his twelve sons promise that they would not leave him buried in Egypt but that they would take his body with them when they returned to Canaan. So his preparation for burial was significant. We read:

> And Joseph fell upon his father's face and wept upon him, and kissed him.
>
> And Joseph commanded his servants the physicians to embalm his father; and the physicians embalmed Israel.
>
> And forty days were fulfilled for him; for so are fulfilled the days of those which are embalmed: and the Egyptians mourned for him threescore and ten days. (Genesis 50:1–3)

The Savior and His Preparations

After the Savior's baptism, He went into the wilderness in preparation for His mortal ministry. Reading the King James Version of Matthew 4:1 gives the idea that being tempted of the devil was the reason Jesus went there. However, Joseph Smith changed that verse to read that Jesus went into the wilderness to be with God. What He does there surely prepares Him for the path He must tread and the work He alone must do. The two accounts are as follows:

> Then was Jesus led up of the Spirit into the wilderness to be tempted of the devil.
> And when he had fasted forty days and forty nights, he was afterward an hungered. (KJV Matthew 4:1–2).

> Then Jesus was led up of the Spirit, into the wilderness, to be *with God.*
> And when he had fasted forty days and forty nights, *and had communed with God,* he was afterwards an hungered, and was left to be tempted of the devil. (JST, Matthew 4:1–2)

By considering the symbolic use of the number forty in the above verses, more can be felt about what was happening. The Savior's intent, His purpose, and some of the emotion that we as readers should feel, are communicated by the number forty. The Son of God was born among mortal men and now faced an enormous task of teaching, reproving, and redeeming all of His Father's children.

The question of being able to fast for a particular length of time is not nearly as important as the preparation that was taking place. Undoubtedly, the Creator of all things, who has the power over life and death, could go without physical sustenance, if that was His choice and will. Even Moses and others could be given help to go without food or water for forty days (Exodus 34:28;

Deuteronomy 9:9). However, the idea of exactly how long the fast was is not the picture the words paint of the account.

To appreciate the feeling for this event, which displays the enormity of the preparation the Savior underwent, we must first be aware of the symbolism and, second, consider the message of the symbolism within the elements. Finally, the Holy Spirit must be allowed to lead and verify proper understanding. This is the process of reading symbolic language.

Elijah and His Preparation

During the time that Elijah hid from King Ahab and his wife Jezebel because he had challenged things they had done while they occupied the throne, he needed direction from God. He had sealed the heavens, promising the king that "there shall not be dew nor rain these years, but according to my word" (1 Kings 17:1). This had made him a hunted man. He was now to go into Mount Horeb to wait for further directions. His work in the matter of calling King Ahab to repentance and to bring rain back to the land was not yet finished.

The account reads, "And he arose, and did eat and drink, and went in the strength of that meat forty days and forty nights unto Horeb the mount of God" (1 Kings 19:8).

In Horeb, or Mount Sinai, Elijah's preparations for his further mission to Israel and to other nations were completed.

The Children of Israel Suffered and Needed to Prepare

Upon fleeing Egypt, the Israelites were not ready yet to enter the land promised to them. They needed to be cleansed and prepared. The following scriptures indicate that in addition to cleansing and preparation, the time spent wandering in the wilderness would be full of suffering and hardship:

> And the children of Israel did eat manna forty
> years, until they came to a land inhabited; they did eat
> manna, until they came unto the borders of the land of
> Canaan. (Exodus 16:35)

> And your children shall wander in the wilderness
> forty years, and bear your whoredoms, until your car-
> cases be wasted in the wilderness.
> After the number of the days in which ye searched
> the land, even forty days, each day for a year, shall
> ye bear your iniquities, even forty years, and ye shall
> know my breach of promise. (Numbers 14:33–34)

Moses was directed to send spies into the land. For how long
were they gone? "And they returned from searching of the land
after forty days" (Numbers 13:25).

Forty Years in the Wilderness

New archaeological discoveries shed light on the time the children of Israel actually spent wandering in the wilderness. These
recent finds indicate that the Israelites made inroads and habita-
tions into Canaan long before the forty years were finished after
they left their bondage in Egypt. Such discoveries can be troublesome if we read the account like Westerners without taking into
consideration the figurative meanings. Note these verses:

> And thou shalt remember all the way which the
> Lord thy God led thee these forty years in the wilder-
> ness, to humble thee, and to prove thee, to know what
> was in thine heart, whether thou wouldest keep his
> commandments, or no. (Deuteronomy 8:2)

> But with whom was he grieved forty years? Was it
> not with them that had sinned, whose carcases fell in
> the wilderness? (Hebrews 3:17)

Some of the conflicts and difficulties of the accounts vanish when we understand that God wanted to cleanse and prepare His people to enter the promised land. They were people who had to suffer through tribulation because of their disobedience to commandments and directions from God. Therefore, they had to wait forty years, or a period of undetermined length, which was to them and to all who knew of them, a period of affliction, suffering, cleansing, and preparation.

Today, We Say Things in the Same Way

Today, we use numbers to transmit feeling and meaning in our expressions. We might say, "I've said I'm sorry dozens of times!" Or, "If I've said it once, I've said it a hundred times!" In expressions such as these, the number is not as critical as the intent, the depth of emotion, and the feelings of the situation.

This is the same kind of a message as when someone tells you that you missed the target by a mile, even though your arrow or shot passed within a few inches or feet of the objective. Listeners will never know exactly how close you came if you say, "I missed that car by a hair." Similarly, when someone tells you she is in seventh heaven, she has told you how she feels by using a single, symbolic number.

The Story of the Twins—Jacob and Esau

The account of Jacob and Esau, which uses the word *forty*, tells of the conflict between these two brothers. The situation first deals with the life of Esau, Jacob's older twin brother. He chose to marry out of the covenant and against the wishes of his parents:

> And Esau was forty years old when he took to wife Judith the daughter of Beeri the Hittite, and Bashemath the daughter of Elon the Hittite: Which were a grief of mind to Isaac and to Rebekah. (Genesis 26:34–35)

Marriagable age in biblical times did not differ drastically from the average age of marriage today ("Everyday Life" in Bible Times, *National Geographic*, 305), so it seems a bit unusual for Esau not to be married at an earlier age. Also, we note that the age mentioned is once again not forty-one or thirty-nine but forty.

Looking at the message in verse 34, Esau was ready for marriage in age but not in wisdom. Therefore, verse 35 records the grief of his parents, not because he married too old or too young but because of the immaturity and the poor choices he had made. His choices added to the suffering and punishment that came into his life and the lives of his parents.

Likewise, the book of Genesis notes that Isaac was a similar age when he married. "And Isaac was forty years old when he took Rebekah to wife, the daughter of Bethuel the Syrian of Padanaram, the sister to Laban the Syrian" (Genesis 25:20).

Generally, the reader of the biblical story passes it off as coincidence that these two men, father and son, both had the age of their marriage mentioned, and that both married at age forty. If this information was included in the account because of the coincidence and unusualness of the two events, it would seem more logical that something such as the following should have been written: "And Esau was forty years old, just like his father, when he took to wife"

But this is beyond coincidence. It was put there with the idea that all who read would understand something about the men and what they did in fulfilling the necessary preparations prior to their marriage.

As We Approach God

When we approach the house of God to worship, one of the most important thoughts should be of our own worthiness to draw near to God. Such a message could be related to one's consciousness if certain physical symbols were present and known. The temple Solomon was commanded to construct had two features that had the number forty in their description. One of the measurements was for the temple itself: "And the house, that is, the temple before it, was forty cubits long" (1 Kings 6:17).

The other measurement was for the lavers within the holy place of worship, the containers that held water to be used for cleansing burnt offerings. Each laver contained forty baths of water (1 Kings 7:38).

The outside walls of the tabernacle built by Moses, which was the precursor to the temple built by Solomon, also had features using forty. The walls of the tabernacle suggest the message of cleansing and preparation because instructions regarding their construction included the symbolic number forty: "And thou shalt make forty sockets of silver under the twenty boards; two sockets under one board for his two tenons, and two sockets under another board for his two tenons" (Exodus 26:19).

The use of numbers is both practical and logical in these applications; however, that is also the manner in which symbols and types are couched. They seem practical and standard to most, but to others they offer meaning and messages that sustain and inspire action and commitment.

Such is the next illustration as well. It is not biblical. It doesn't fall in the category of Eastern or ancient writing. It comes in direction from God to the prophet of the restoration to build the Kirtland Temple: "Let my servant Joseph Smith, Jun., have appointed unto him the lot which is laid off for the building of my house, which is forty rods long and twelve wide, and also the inheritance upon which his father now resides" (D&C 104:43).

The message of the number twelve (priesthood) combining with the number forty (preparation and cleansing) seems significant. Imagine the feelings that could come to the mind of someone who approaches a place of worship who knows the message of forty and knows that the place of worship is labeled with forty.

The block on which the Salt Lake Temple stands, commonly called "Temple Square," was laid out in 1847 after the pattern for cities of Zion. It is still forty rods on each side, or forty rods squared.

Amplifying the Numbers

When one understands the use of numbers and the message they convey, it is not difficult to add to that idea the practice of amplifying that message by adding another digit to the number. This doesn't change the message of the number but simply amplifies it. Such an amplification would multiply forty by ten, thus making it four hundred.

This idea of amplification of the number helps solve some scriptural inconsistencies. The following is an example: "Now the sojourning of the children of Israel, who dwelt in Egypt, was four hundred and thirty years" (Exodus 12:40).

The Alexandrian copy of the Septuagint agrees with the King James version. It reads, "Now the sojourning of the children of Israel, and of their fathers, which they sojourned in the land of Canaan and in the land of Egypt, was 430 years" (see Clark's *Bible Commentary*, 1: 356).

The Apostle Paul also notes this same time period: "This I say, that the covenant, that was confirmed before of God in Christ, the law, which was four hundred and thirty years after, cannot disannul, that it should make the promise of none effect" (Galatians 3:17).

Now consider the apparent inconsistency: Abraham, grandfather to Jacob, was told in prophecy that his descendants would be in a land that was not theirs for four hundred years.

> And he said unto Abram, Know of a surety that thy seed shall be a stranger in a land that is not theirs, and shall serve them; and they shall afflict them four hundred years; and also that nation, whom they shall serve, will I judge: and afterward shall they come out with great substance. (Genesis 15:13–14)

This historical period is noted in Acts with a similar indication of time:

> And God spake on this wise, That his seed should

sojourn in a strange land; and that they should bring them into bondage, and entreat them evil four hundred years. And the nation to whom they shall be in bondage will I judge, said God: and after that shall they come forth, and serve me in this place. (Acts 7:6–7)

To some, the loss of thirty years seems insignificant. The question, however, still remains about why the number is remembered and recorded with different counts. Notice the words and message that appear in the verses just cited in Acts and Genesis. The messages of punishment, preparation, hardship, and cleansing are dominant. That is what the reader should get out of those verses. Even if the number of years would be only near forty, its significance could still have given the same message as the amplified number of forty multiplied by ten.

There is no conflict when the message we look for is what their sojourn was going to be like and what they were told beforehand as a warning. They were told that their children and their children's children would live difficult lives in a strange land because of their disobedience, and that they would be there until they had cleansed themselves and prepared themselves to come back to the land God had promised. This seems more important for them to know than exactly how many years this sojourn would be endured.

The count given for the number prepared for war in Joshua's time may well also fall into this same category of amplification of the symbolic number. The account reads: "About forty thousand prepared for war passed over before the Lord unto battle, to the plains of Jericho" (Joshua 4:13).

Jacob and Esau Story Amplified

Not only does the record state that Esau was forty years old when he wed, but it also tells when Jacob, his twin brother, returned many years later, having gained wealth and posterity. Jacob had received the birthright from Esau by deceit, and he was afraid to come again to his brother. Yet, it seems, his brother was waiting anxiously for his time of accounting with Jacob. The account reads:

> And Jacob lifted up his eyes, and looked, and, behold, Esau came, and with him four hundred men. And he divided the children unto Leah, and unto Rachel, and unto the two handmaids.
>
> And he put the handmaids and their children foremost, and Leah and her children after, and Rachel and Joseph hindermost.
>
> And he passed over before them, and bowed himself to the ground seven times, until he came near to his brother. (Genesis 33:1–3)

When Jacob saw the men, did he know there were four hundred? Were there exactly four hundred? Why would the record mention the number? Could it not have simply said that there were hundreds of men?

However, applying what we understand about this number, Jacob perceived that his brother was going to, or was in a position to, punish him or make him suffer. That is why he positioned his family and possessions the way he did, to try and affect the feelings of Esau. Now that number means a great deal more when put into that context. Yes, there were a lot of men, but Jacob sees them for what they were or could be to him—a punishment.

As Physical Punishment

Under the Law of Moses and other councils of discipline, the number of lashes given as punishment was forty. What an association of thought with a number! In Deuteronomy, we read the law: "Forty stripes he may give him, and not exceed: lest, if he should exceed, and beat him above these with many stripes, then thy brother should seem vile unto thee" (Deuteronomy 25:3).

To be certain that they never exceeded the law, forty lashes, less one, were administered. Still, it is interesting that the number of lashes associated with punishment is not thirty-nine but forty.

The Apostle Paul said of his suffering, "Of the Jews five times received I forty stripes save one" (2 Corinthians 11:2). In his case, evidently a count was taken and noted. However, there is a message in addition to the actual times one was struck. The number forty only had to cross the lips or be picked up by the ear, and there came to mind the message of suffering and punishment.

Times of Oppression from Rulers and Nations

Many times, the number forty is used to indicate the unrighteous or oppressive reign of a king or nation. Some of these instances follow:

> And the children of Israel did evil again in the sight of the Lord; and the Lord delivered them into the hand of the Philistines forty years. (Judges 13:1)

> And it came to pass, when he made mention of the ark of God, that he fell from off the seat backward by the side of the gate, and his neck brake, and he died: for he was an old man, and heavy. And he had judged Israel forty years. (1 Samuel 4:18)

> And the Philistine drew near morning and evening, and presented himself forty days. (1 Samuel 17:16)

> And it came to pass after forty years, that Absalom said unto the king, I pray thee, let me go and pay my vow, which I have vowed unto the Lord, in Hebron. (2 Samuel 15:7)

Other scriptural examples of possible symbolic use of the number forty for punishing include Acts 13:21 and 23:13, 21 and Ezekiel 4:6 and 29:11–13.

Forty Never Used to Tell of Happiness

In addition, no times exist in the scriptures when the number forty is used in any relationship with happiness, freedom, or times of plenty. It is not used to tell of righteous reigns, births, or times free from oppression. This finding is powerful and helpful in reaching conclusions about the number forty.

Certainly, this realization only adds to the idea that the number forty symbolizes preparation, cleansing, suffering, and affliction.

How Long Do We Live?

Without understanding the symbolic use of numbers and how they can be combined, a reader would be left to wonder about such verses as Moses 8:16–17, which reads:

> And it came to pass that Noah prophesied, and taught the things of God, even as it was in the beginning.
>
> And the Lord said unto Noah: My Spirit shall not always strive with man, for he shall know that all flesh shall die; yet his days shall be an hundred and twenty years; and if men do not repent, I will send in the floods upon them.

What does it mean that man's days will be a hundred and twenty years? Few of us reach that ripe old age, although a very few have exceeded it. Certainly, the number of years seems to vary from one civilization to another. Today, the average age life expectancy has reached a level only dreamed of in past millennia. Still, almost all lives end short of one hundred twenty years.

However, by applying one of the symbolic messages of the number forty, that of preparation, and combining that with the number three, which denotes fullness, we can see a marvelous purpose for this life's work. It is that we can be fully prepared to move on to what was revealed to Abraham when he recorded:

We will go down, for there is space there, and we will take of these materials, and we will make an earth whereon these may dwell;

And we will prove them herewith, to see if they will do all things whatsoever the Lord their God shall command them;

And they who keep their first estate shall be added upon; and they who keep not their first estate shall not have glory in the same kingdom with those who keep their first estate; and they who keep their second estate shall have glory added upon their heads for ever and ever." (Abraham 3:24–26)

Saying that the time of our lives here on earth is to be one hundred and twenty years, or three times forty, seems a marvelous statement of truth and explanation. It is an idiomatic phrase, however, and we need to understand it as such.

The Book of Mormon and Forty

If the Bible is an Eastern or Oriental book, what about the Book of Mormon? Even though this book was first translated and published in America, we know that its writers were of Eastern origin and spoke and wrote in Eastern languages (1 Nephi 1:2). The Book of Mormon should thus have many of these same Eastern characteristics woven into its historical and doctrinal accounts.

When the story is recorded of Ammon and the sixteen strong men who looked for the land of Lehi-Nephi, we realize that the group is lost. They set out on a mission of concern, looking out for the well-being of fellow citizens and relatives who had traveled to a land they had previously inhabited. No report had been received from this group, and so Ammon and his companions were commissioned to find them.

The description of the time Ammon and his men wandered is interesting:

> And now, they knew not the course they should travel in the wilderness to go up to the land of Lehi-Nephi; therefore they wandered *many days* in the wilderness, even *forty days* did they wander.
>
> And when they had wandered *forty days* they came to a hill which is north of the land of Shilom, and there they pitched their tents. (Mosiah 7:4–5; emphasis added)

Once again, we ask ourselves whether the writer was trying to tell us exactly how many days, or whether he was trying to tell of the suffering and the associating feelings that must have come to them as well?

In the next illustration, Nephi may be indicating the chronological number of years that had passed, but consistent with the use of the number forty, he did not use this number to convey happiness, freedom, and contentment. Instead, he writes, "And it sufficeth me to say that forty years had passed away, and we had already had wars and contentions with our brethren" (2 Nephi 5:34).

Conclusion

Many times, the number forty is used to give a count, telling how many. However, more often than not, we should recognize that the number forty communicates the message of affliction, preparation, suffering, or cleansing. This number is one of the most used symbolic numbers that we observe in scriptural texts. We see it frequently, and when it is used, we consider first its symbolic value and then, when no single symbolism or dualism is noted, it should be considered for its literal, or numerical, value.

Conclusion

The Bible itself is evidence that numbers were significant to those who wrote as well as to those who compiled the written word. The King James scholars studied its books not just for their own edification but so they could decide which writings should be included within the collection.

Other versions of the Bible include additional books or transcripts, such as Tobit and 1 and 2 Maccabees. However, the King James scholars seem to have had an objective that may well have been centered in a message of its numbers. An understanding of their symbolism provides insight into the result of their final choices.

Sixty-three books were to be included. At present printing, however, the King James Bible contains sixty-six books. The reason for the difference is that the books of Samuel, Kings, and Chronicles have been divided into two books each. Careful examination of the titles of these books tells, in part, the thought relative to the naming of these records. Having two books each was influenced by the Greek Septuagint. So there are really sixty-three books in the entire Bible.

As one last exercise, let's look at the number sixty-three. The factors of the number sixty-three are three, seven, and nine. Nine, of course, is the square of the number three. Nine stands by itself with the message of judgment, or it can be thought of as the square of three, the number for fullness. Seven sends a message of perfection. Combining the ideas of fullness, judgment, and perfection results in a powerful way to approach and feel about the Bible as a whole.

The Bible is divided into two parts: the Old Testament and

the New Testament. The number two suggests testimony, and that is exactly what each of them is meant to be—a testament. One is old, the other new, but both testify of the same God, the same atoning promise, and the same reward for righteousness.

The Old Testament contains thirty-nine books, although if you consider Samuel, Kings, and Chronicles as one book each, it actually has only thirty-six books. And what are the factors for the number thirty-six? They can be four and nine, numbers that send messages of universality and judgment, numbers that combine to make a powerful image.

Two other factors are three and twelve. These numbers give the message of fullness and priesthood. When the messages of these numbers are combined, they reflect a powerful way to feel about the record of the Old Testament.

Finally, the New Testament contains twenty-seven books. What are the factors of this number? We find no possibilities other than the number three, squared and cubed—a significant symbol. No less significant, however, than the New Testament itself, a record of the fulfillment of all the prophets who looked forward to, saw, spoke, and testified of the coming of the Messiah. Their testimony does not just have length and width, it has height and depth. It is full and cubed, truly a testament of God, manifesting Himself and doing so in total fullness.

How should we feel about looking for symbols, things that witness because of their innate nature? Moses recorded what he was told by the Lord: "Behold, all things have their likeness, and all things are created and made to bear record of me, both things which are temporal, and things which are spiritual; things which are in the heavens above, and things which are on the earth, and things which are in the earth, and things which are under the earth, both above and beneath: all things bear record of me" (Moses 6:63).

If all things are created and made to bear record of God, surely the possibility exists that numbers bear record of Him. Numbers have been an essential element of every civilization and language. Abundant evidence exists that the writers of the scriptural texts, as well as the compilers, intended that the message of certain numbers would illustrate and amplify the messages of their words. I have discovered such evidence, and I want to be a part of that of which Moses wrote. I want to be a witness of God. I want to bear record of God and what He has done.

I hope this writing is pleasing to God. I hope it bears testimony of the things God has done as well as the way we should feel about Him. I believe there are far more things that testify of God and His work within the scriptural text than are generally identified as such. I hope this writing helps in this recognition process, the process of experiencing the symbolic messages of numbers that are contained in the words of God and His prophets.

Sources

Books

Barber, Allen H. *Celestial Symbols.* Bountiful, Utah: Horizon, 1989.

Brewer, Cobham E. *Brewer's Dictionary,* 1810–1897. Dictionary of Phrase and Fable, 1894.

Bullinger, E. W. *Number in Scripture.* Grand Rapids, Mich.: Kregel, 1967.

Clark, Adam. *Clark's Bible Commentary.* 6 vols. London: 1844.

Draper, Richard D. *Opening the Seven Seals.* Salt Lake City: Deseret Book, 1991.

Everyday Life in Bible Times. Washington, D.C.: National Geographic, 1967.

Fairbairn, Patrick D. *The Teachers and Students Bible Encyclopedia.* Toledo, Ohio: Browning Dixon, 1902.

Grant, F. W. *The Numerical Bible.* London: Loizeaux, 1890.

Hafen, Bruce C. *The Broken Heart.* Salt Lake City: Deseret Book 1989.

Kaiser, Walter C. *Hard Sayings of the Bible.* Downer's Grove, Ill.: InterVarsity Press, 1996.

The Latter-day Saints' Millennial Star. Manchester, London, and Liverpool, England: The Church of Jesus Christ of Latter-day Saints, 1840–1970.

McConkie, Bruce R. *A New Witness for the Articles of Faith.* Salt Lake City: Deseret Book, 1980.

———. *Mormon Doctrine.* 2d ed. Salt Lake City: Bookcraft, 1966.

McConkie, Joseph Fielding, and Donald W. Parry. *A Guide to Scriptural Symbols.* Salt Lake City: Bookcraft, 1990.

McKay, David O. *Cherished Experiences from the Writings of President David O. McKay.* Compiled by Clare Middlemiss. Salt Lake City: Deseret Book, 1955.

Nibley, Hugh B. *Mormonism and Early Christianity.* Salt Lake City: Deseret Book, 1970.

Orr, James. *The International Standard Bible Encyclopedia.* Grand Rapids, Mich.: Eerdmans, 1946.

Petersen, Mark E. *Moses, Man of Miracles.* Salt Lake City: Deseret Book, 1985.

Smith, Joseph, Jr. *Lectures on Faith.* Salt Lake City: Deseret Book, 1985.

Smith, William. *Smith's Bible Dictionary.* Grand Rapids, Mich.: Zondervan Publishing House, 1948.

Teachers and Students' Bible Encyclopedia. 5 vols. Toledo, Ohio: Browning and Dixon, 1902.

Unger, Merrill F. *Unger's Concise Bible Dictionary.* Grand Rapids, Mich.: Baker Book House, 1957.

Vallowe, Ed. F. *Biblical Mathematics.* Columbia, S.C.: Olive Press, 1997.

———. *Biblical Mathematics—Keys to Scripture Numerics.* Forest Park, Georgia: Ed. F. Vallowe Evangelistic Association, 1988.

Articles

Angel, Truman O. "The Salt Lake City Temple." *Millennial Star* 36, no. 18 (5 May 1874): 274–75.

Kalinowski, Edward. "Numbers in the Bible." *Cromwell, Homiletic & Pastoral Review,* January 2000.

Lund, Gerald N. "Understanding Scriptural Symbols." *Ensign,* October 1986, 22–26.

Machlin, Milt. "Joshua and the Archeologist." *Reader's Digest,* September 1990, 135–39.

Millet, Robert L. "The Birth of the Messiah: A Closer Look at the Infancy Narrative of Matthew." CES Symposium, August 1980.

Thomasson, Gordon. "Mytonomy and the Book of Mormon," *Insights,* June 1984, 1.

Tuttle, A. Theodore. "The Pearl of Great Price as Scripture." BYU Sperry Symposium, June 1982.

Welch, John W. "Counting to Ten." *Journal of Book of Mormon Studies* 12 (November 2003): 43–57.

About the Author

George M. Peacock grew up in Orangeville, Utah. He has sought answers to scriptural questions throughout his life, beginning with his service as a full-time missionary to Independence, Missouri. His area of labor later included much of the Bible Belt.

After his mission he earned a bachelor's degree in secondary education and a master's degree in religious education, both from Brigham Young University. He began teaching in the Church Educational System in 1964, retiring in 2000. In addition to teaching seminary and institute classes, he fulfilled assignments in both administration and teacher improvement.

George married Arlene Christensen of Meridian, Idaho, in 1963. They are the parents of five married children who reside near their parents in St. George, Utah. George and Arlene serve as workers in the St. George Temple.